African Trade Beads

THEIR 10,000-YEAR

HISTORY

ISSA TRAORE

D1520531

FIREFLY BOOKS

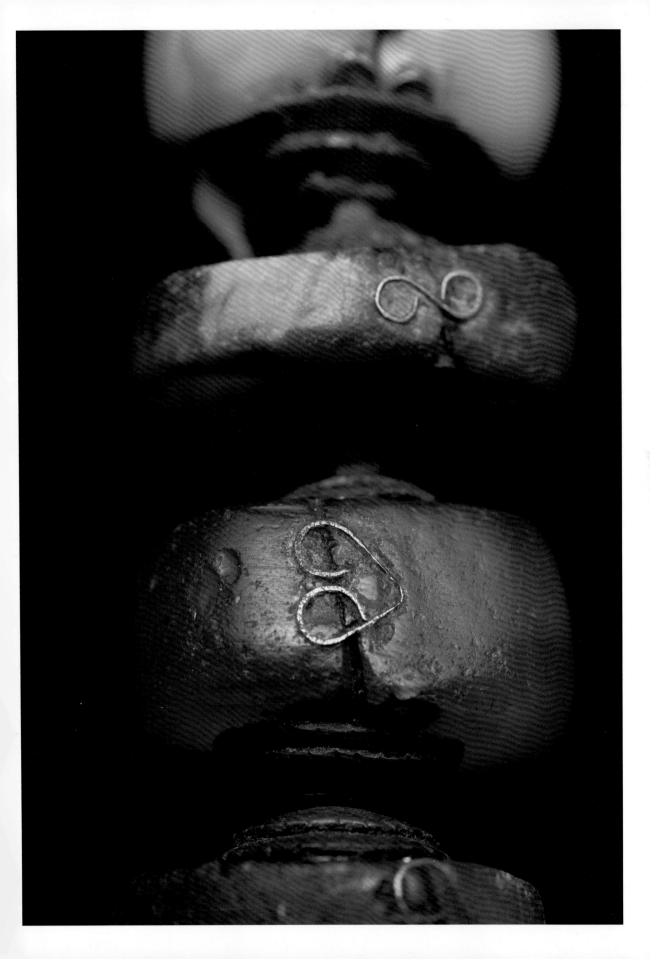

Preface

My relationship with glass beads is like my relationship with
my family. My father used to be a glass bead dealer and my
paternal grandfather ran an old-fashioned antique shop called
a *Marabaka*. My father said that in the past there were lots of
beads. For example, amber beads were separated by size and
then sold in 50-kilogram rice bags. After dealers got them, they
would occasionally thread the beads together, if they had
time, thus creating strings of beads. Growing up in this type of
environment meant that I was in close contact with many old
glass beads since childhood. Glass beads felt like siblings to me.

I am originally from Bamako, Mali, but I have been living in
Japan for about 20 years. In this book, I will introduce you to
African glass beads (known as *Konon*). Most of the *Konon* featured
here were obtained in Mali, so let me first provide a brief
introduction to my home country.

The Republic of Mali is located in West Africa and covers
approximately 1,241,000 square kilometers. It has a population
of around 21 million. It is a landlocked country that shares its
borders with seven other nations. Two-thirds of its territory
consists of the Sahara Desert, the rest being savanna. The
majority of its population resides in the south. The country's
name is derived from the Mali Empire, a historical empire that
emerged in the 13th century in West Africa and reached its zenith
during the reign of Mansa Musa, between 1312 and 1337.

It is actually extremely difficult to obtain a single string of
popular *Konon* from one place, even if you search throughout a
number of local areas.

Villages in these local areas continue to have thriving weekly
markets. These markets offer a wide range of products, from
daily essentials to food items, livestock, antiques, and used
goods. They function essentially as flea markets. Antique beads
were often available in these markets.

Dealers from different villages and neighboring areas come
together on specific days of the week to open markets. For
example, the market found in Djenné takes place on Mondays.
Those in Bandiagara, the capital of the Dogon tribe (which
operates like a major regional city), are held twice a week
on Mondays and Fridays. Bankas Village hosts its market on
Tuesdays. The villages of Sangha, Ningari, and Dourou rotate

Konon... Glass beads
Marabaka... Antique dealer

Both from the Bamanan
language of Mali.

their markets every five days. This method of joint participation leads to larger markets and thus attracts a greater number of visitors.

The Dogon week used to consist of five days instead of seven. Markets are thus held every five days as a vestige of that tradition.

In Mopti, the largest market takes place on Thursdays. It's famous for livestock, and visitors come from as far away as the neighboring country of Burkina Faso in search of cattle. Bandiagara Escarpment, home to the Dogon tribe, and Djenné both belong to the Mopti region. When visiting rural towns in Mali, Burkina Faso, Côte d'Ivoire, and other countries nearby, you should schedule your trip to coincide with market days. The markets are vibrant and feel almost like festivals.

Ever since I was in high school, I have been visiting the local markets in search of glass beads. Bamako is quite far away though, so I would stay in a handful of villages over a span of several weeks while exploring the markets. During these visits, I would stay with acquaintances or in the homes of *Marabaka* (antique shop owners) who were introduced to me by others.

When I was young there were still many *Konon* available locally. They were brought in from the countryside in abundance. I would count them, help thread them, and, when foreign visitors arrived, I would arrange the *Konon* by type. Over the years, I noticed that the quantity of *Konon* I encountered was decreasing, and their quality was declining while their value was steadily rising.

When I was young, I once asked my father, "Why do foreigners buy *Konon Koro* (antique beads) at such high prices?"

My father replied, "Some *Konon Koro* are over a thousand years old, others are several hundred years old. Nowadays, people can make cars and airplanes, but they can't create old beads like these." He then picked up a seven-layer genesis chevron and a six-layer second-generation chevron* and said, "Most people would choose this beautiful six-layer bead without really comparing it with any other beads. Only a few would be captivated by this seven-layer bead. I would suggest that whenever you come across *any* antique beads, not just chevrons, you should really observe them closely. They are all unique

*Note: This book considers Egyptian-made glass with seven layers – referred to as genesis chevron – to be first-generation, while Venetian-made six-layer chevron beads are second-generation (see p. 124).

and beautiful!" His words were one of the catalysts behind my interest in *Konon*.

When I thought back on my father's stories about the old days and sacks full of *Konon*, I decide that, even if the quantity was small and the quality far from perfect, I should still try to collect *Konon*, little-by-little, within my means.

Certainly, random antique beads can still be found in abundance. However, once you look closely at their color, shape, and pattern, you'll note that there are quite a few beads that you'll never find offered for sale. No matter what kind of collector you are, there are beads that you just can't acquire, despite having seen them in museums or books.

I recall an incident while attending a bead show in Germany. There were certain beads at this show that had become quite rare in Mali and, despite my finest negotiating, I couldn't buy them. Finally, on the last day of the show, I decided to trade a large quantity of my own beads for them. A friend who was with me said, "No matter how good these beads are, if you pay such a high price, they'll never sell." I replied, "These beads aren't actually for sale. They are for my private collection. I admit that I am getting the short end of the stick here, but the beads I obtained have become really rare in Mali." Honestly, those beads were quite valuable to me, but my friend laughed and thought I was foolish.

Whenever I returned from local markets, I would always set aside some *Konon* as "not of sale." I just kept them as part of my personal collection.

I've wanted to collect *Konon* ever since I was young. I hope to someday build a bead museum in Africa, a place where people – both Africans and foreign tourists – can see the role that beads played in the history of mankind, right there in the heart of Africa. If the cradle of humanity is in Africa, then the homeland of beads is in Africa too! I really do believe that there are beads in Africa that must be preserved (and that some of them must also remain in Africa). Before realizing my dream of building a bead museum in Africa, I want to introduce a larger audience to the allure of African *Konon* with this book.

These beads were obtained in
rural Mali before coming to Japan,
and they have been kept in their
original state.

Contents

Special Features

LEGEND

- In this book the terms "beads," "glass beads," and "gems" are used interchangeably.
- Photo specifications are (top down): size, ethnic use group, and country of acquisition.
- Beads are measured in millimeters (inches in brackets).
- Unless otherwise specified, measurements are taken from the central bead. In cases where several strings are stacked together, the measurement is taken from the central bead on the outside string.
- Clusters of the same type of beads are referred to as "a string of beads." These are collections of beads of the same type put together by dealers. Particularly rare beads are put together and marked as "collectible necklaces." Accessories used locally are labeled as necklaces or bracelets.
- Trade Beads (2) may contain beads from different production countries than the headings suggest. They are just grouped together for presentation.
- The term "Bamanan tribe" refers to the more common Bambara tribe. Bambara originated from the French colonial era, so in this book, the self-designation of the local people in Mali – Bamanan – is used.

The History of Beads and Their African Counterparts

THE OLDEST BEADS

Generally, beads are considered to be "small, perforated objects with a string passed through," but the oldest "beads" discovered to date are actually made from shells. Dyed bivalve shell beads have been found in the Cave of Los Aviones in southern Spain, while spiral shell beads were discovered in the Skhul Cave along the Mediterranean coast of Israel. They date back nearly 120,000 years.

Shell beads made from Nassa mud snails, called Tick Shells (*Nassarius kraussianus*), dating back 100,000 to 70,000 years ago, were found in archaeological sites in North Africa. In the Blombos Cave in South Africa, around 70 such beads made from Nassa mud snails have been discovered. Of these, 24 were found clustered together in one location, suggesting that they were held together with a string.

In East Africa, conus shell beads dating back around 65,000 years were unearthed in the Panga ya Saidi Cave near the Kenyan coast. In northern Tanzania, near the Mumba Rock Shelter, beads made from ostrich eggshell – dating back approximately 49,000 years – have been found. These are considered to be the oldest ostrich eggshell beads on earth.

BEAD MATERIALS

In the Paleolithic era, people would create decorative items with the bones, antlers, and hides of animals after eating the meat. Decorations made from animal parts were believed to bestow the courage and strength of the animal upon the wearer. Additionally, by altering the skeletal structure of the animal through the carving or engraving of bones, it was believed that one could enhance the inherent magic or power that the animal possessed.

In coastal regions, seashells were likely collected for use in crafting ornaments, but certain items were also fashioned from other raw materials, like nuts and seeds.

Around 10,000 years ago, during the Neolithic era, people began using stones for beads. While processing stones for this purpose was challenging, the resulting beads were durable and resistant to decay. They were lustrous, came in various colors, were homogeneous in texture, had smooth surfaces, and could be shaped as desired.

During these early stages, natural materials – like the bones, tusks, teeth, shells, eggshells, nuts, and seeds mentioned above – were combined with stones to create beads.

Today, most people think of glass when they think of beads. However, before beads were made entirely of glass there was a type of bead that used other substances for a core and then applied a glassy coating (glaze) to their surface. The first type of glazed beads used stones – like cryolite, quartz, crystal, carnelian, obsidian, agate, feldspar, etc. – for their core. The second type were made with a mixture of fired quartz micrograins (faience). Both types began to be produced in Mesopotamia and Egypt around 4100 BCE.

Beads made completely from glass are believed to have originated in Mesopotamia around 2500 BCE. It's also thought that bead making specifically for human adornment began at this time. With the advent of glass, thought to be the first man-made material, the shapes and designs of beads evolved dramatically. Beads became a central element of trade and spread throughout the world in later periods.

Early glass was often produced in dark colors due to the fact that it was originally crafted to imitate precious stones. Cobalt oxide-containing blue glass, which imitates lapis lazuli, is a prime example of this. Glass could intentionally replicate rare gemstones while also possessing the advantage of malleability when compared to mined stones. Additionally, glass required no polishing, which further solidified its status as prime bead material.

AFRICAN BEADS

It is important to consider geographical influences when attempting to understand African beads. The African continent is comprised of a great variety of environments, including deserts, tropical rainforests, temperate forests, savannas, fertile plains, and more. Natural resources are distributed unevenly across these regions, and economic, political, and religious systems reflect differences in the natural environment. Those who possessed valuable resources like gold or ivory often encouraged the development of art and craftsmanship as both a means to visually express their power and to act as offerings to appease the gods. Beadwork also played a role in distinguishing rulers from the general population. The elaborate beadwork crafted by specialized artisans for the Yoruba kings is much more intricate than that made by East African pastoralist groups like the

Pokot and Samburu for personal use. Beads were seen as essential elements in the lives of the latter and were worn to signify age, marital status, and social standing.

Beads served as an essential communication system in all African societies. Bead adornment acted as a language expressing social class, religion, politics, and artistic attitudes. They came to truly embody the identity of various ethnic groups.

The people of Africa have had access to a vast array of raw bead materials from their rich lands for centuries. Organic materials such as shells, seeds, nuts, bones, tusks, and teeth were widely used as ornaments, while stones – although more labor intensive to collect and process – became attractive bead materials.

Cowrie shells, appreciated for their durability and shape (vertical symbolizing female fertility and horizontal representing eyes) have also had a long history in Africa. They were used as burial offerings over 10,000 years ago, but they also served as currency in certain places until the 20th century.

The production of stone beads in sub-Saharan Africa was limited to certain regions. Around 1000 BCE, in the Nok culture of Nigeria, various types of stone beads were crafted, including tubular and double-drilled. In the 15th century, the Benin Kingdom saw the development of stone bead production, heavily encouraged by the king. Benin artisans became experts at carving stone beads for the royal family.

Beads held great importance in Benin, where royal beadwork gradually became more sophisticated. Seventeenth-century royal official attire often featured coral bead costumes, including skirts, shirts, crowns, and staffs. A stone bead industry has also been shown to exist in Ilorin, Nigeria. Merchants from Arabia and Sudan introduced materials like agate, carnelian, red jasper – as well as old stones – to Ilorin. There, local artisans processed them into beads.

The history of metal beads in Africa is somewhat unclear. Iron had been used for tools and weapons since around 300 BCE, but its use in jewelry appears to be a more recent phenomenon. However, tin beads in the shape of shells were discovered in Nok archaeological sites dating back to approximately 1000 BCE. European explorers arriving in West Africa in the early 15th century noted the presence of gold jewelry, such as bead necklaces and bracelets. Much of the gold jewelry in West Africa was crafted by the Ashanti tribe using the "lost-wax" casting method. This technique had been known in West Africa since around the 9th century and is believed to have been transmitted from North Africa through trans-Saharan trade routes. Sudanese mines supplied resources to gem traders in Ancient Egypt during the Old Kingdom period, and during the New Kingdom period even more gold came from the south of Sudan. In the Middle Ages, both the Islamic world in West Asia and the Christian world in Europe began to seek African gold.

THE BEGINNINGS OF TRADE

Prior to the Age of Exploration in the 15th century, when Europe began its global expansion, long-distance trade had already developed in Africa through two major trade networks: the Trans-Saharan and Indian Ocean.

Trade between India and Southeastern Africa had been occurring from around 150 BCE to 200 CE, and among the trade goods were Indian-made glass beads. Beads from that era have been discovered in places like Kilwa and Zanzibar in Tanzania, Sofala in Mozambique, and Madagascar.

In the 7th century, Muslims conquered North Africa and began exchanging brass, cloth, stones, glass beads, Baltic amber, and more for West African gold and ivory. From the 8th century to the 16th century, Islamic empires emerged in West Africa, leading to significant trade relationships. The most prominent states were the Ghana Empire, dominant from the 8th century through the 11th century, and the Mali Empire, spanning the 12th century to the 13th century and extending from the Atlantic to the bend of the Niger River. Mali's capital, Timbuktu, prospered greatly through trade with North Africa. By the 15th century, the Songhai Empire rose to prominence, with Gao as its capital. Many glass beads, serving as evidence of trade beyond the Sahara Desert from North Africa, have been discovered in the ruins of cities like Djenné, which served as vital trade hubs.

TRADE WITH EUROPE

The European glass bead industry from the Renaissance to the 20th century is perhaps the most important part of African bead history. During this period, most explorers,

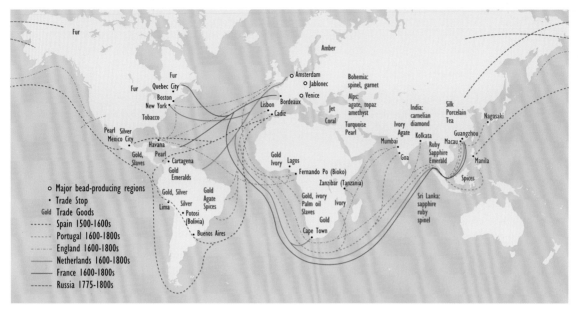

European trade routes 1500–1800s

Reference: Lois Sherr Dubin, *The History of Beads: From 30,000 B.C. to the Present*, Harry N. Abrams, 1987

merchants, and missionaries carried glass beads as gifts and objects of barter, which led to the opening of new markets. The abundance of new markets resulted in a corresponding significant increase in bead production and a surge in the variety of beads being produced. This, in turn, led to continuous improvements and refinements in manufacturing techniques.

Indonesians and Filipinos coveted stone and European glass beads obtained through "western" merchants in India, the Middle East, and China. Up to this point, glass had been completely unknown in the new markets. Once introduced by Europeans, glass beads were valued as rare luxuries. These small, colorful glass beads were viewed as a welcome alternative to other more demanding, labor-intensive, decorative techniques.

Africa experienced a similar introduction to glass beads. It wasn't until the end of the 15th century that the people of the West African coast began trading with Europe. First came the Portuguese. They were followed by the Dutch, English, French, Belgians, and Germans. They brought beautiful Venetian, Dutch, and Bohemian glass beads to Africa.

Africans traded glass beads for spices, ivory, tortoiseshell, rhino horn, palm oil, coconut oil, wood, iron, and gold. They established a close-knit trade network that transported gold and ivory from the interior to the ports and brought back beads.

Up until the 15th century, beads were primarily made from natural materials or single-colored glass, often imitating precious stones. However, when sparkling glass beads with intricate patterns emerged, one can only imagine the amazement of the African people. A new phenomenon emerged as different ethnic groups competed to collect beads according to their own preferences.

MODERN TO CONTEMPORARY GLASS BEADS, RECYCLED BEADS

In Africa, beads made from recycled glass, called "recycled beads," are now being produced. They are also called "powdered glass beads." The main areas of production are in West Africa: Mauritania, Nigeria, and most importantly, Ghana. The origins of bead manufacturing in Ghana are unknown, but some believe it began as early as 1,000 years ago. Today, the majority of powdered glass beads are produced by Ashanti and Krobo artisans and women. According to legend, the Krobo have been making beads "for a long time," with records of Krobo beads being produced as early as the 1920s. Although archaeological evidence is scant, powdered glass bead making in Ghana is thought to go back even further. Jean Barbot, a French commercial officer who conducted two West African expeditions from 1678 to 1682, mentioned the production of powdered glass beads on the Gold Coast (present-day Ghana) in his work *Barbot on Guinea: The Writings of Jean Barbot on West Africa, 1678–1712*.

Powdered glass beads, as the name implies, are made from finely crushed glass. These recycled beads are made mainly from bottle shards and scrap glass. Various types of glass can be used, including old medicine bottles, cosmetics bottles, tableware, ashtrays, window glass, and even broken glass beads. The glass is crushed into pieces, which are then ground into even smaller pieces in a metal mortar. The quality of the beads depends largely on the fineness of the glass powder. Various kinds of glass, like certain beverage brand bottles, are preferred due to their unique characteristics of high melting points and ease of manipulation. These properties are quite important as powdered glass beads are created using molds made of clay.

Mauritania produces recycled glass beads known as Kiffa beads. Kiffa beads are unique to Mauritania and are made using materials like gum Arabic for bonding. These beads are shaped by hand without the use of molds and are believed to have originated in the 19th century, possibly inspired by ancient glass beads from Fustat. Some suggest that Kiffa beads were made for women of lower castes who couldn't afford expensive antique beads.

Such beads are still being made today, and in Africa many bead artisans continue to thrive.

Beads continue to play an incredibly important role in the daily lives of African people, and in events such as births, coming-of-age ceremonies, weddings, and funerals.

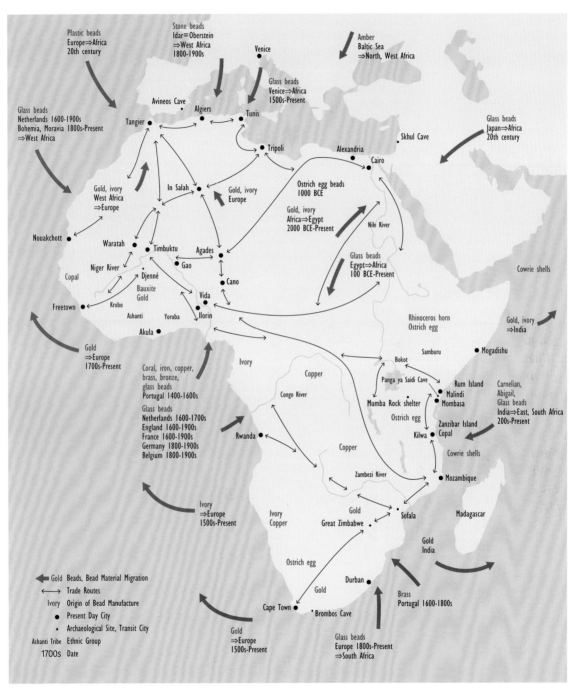

Plastic beads
Europe⇒Africa
20th century

Stone beads
Idar=Oberstein
⇒West Africa
1800-1900s

Venice

Amber
Baltic Sea
⇒North, West Africa

Glass beads
Venice⇒Africa
1500s-Present

Glass beads
Netherlands 1600-1900s
Bohemia, Moravia 1800s-Present
⇒West Africa

Avineos Cave

Algiers

Tunis

Tangier

Tripoli

Alexandria

Cairo

Skhul Cave

Glass beads
Japan⇒Africa
20th century

Gold, ivory
West Africa
⇒Europe

In Salah

Gold, ivory
Europe

Ostrich egg beads
1000 BCE

Gold, ivory
Africa⇒Egypt
2000 BCE-Present

Nile River

Nouakchott

Waratah

Timbuktu

Agades

Glass beads
Egypt⇒Africa
100 BCE-Present

Cowrie shells

Niger River

Gao

Copal

Djenné

Cano

Bauxite
Gold

Freetown

Krobo

Vida

Rhinoceros horn
Ostrich egg

Gold, ivory
⇒India

Ashanti

Yoruba

Ilorin

Akula

Samburu

Mogadishu

Gold
⇒Europe
1700s-Present

Ivory

Bokot

Copper

Coral, iron, copper,
brass, bronze,
glass beads
Portugal 1400-1600s

Congo River

Panga ya Saidi Cave

Rum Island

Malindi

Mombasa

Carnelian,
Abigail,
Glass beads
India⇒East, South Africa
200s-Present

Glass beads
Netherlands 1600-1700s
England 1600-1900s
France 1600-1900s
Germany 1800-1900s
Belgium 1800-1900s

Mumba Rock shelter

Ostrich egg

Zanzibar Island
Copal

Rwanda

Kilwa

Copper

Cowrie shells

Zambezi River

Mozambique

Ivory
⇒Europe
1500s-Present

Ivory
Copper

Gold

Sofala

Madagascar

Great Zimbabwe

Gold
India

Gold Beads, Bead Material Migration

Ostrich egg

Durban

Trade Routes

Gold

Brass
Portugal 1600-1800s

Ivory   Origin of Bead Manufacture

•   Present Day City

·   Archaeological Site, Transit City

Cape Town

Brombos Cave

Ashanti Tribe   Ethnic Group

1700s   Date

Gold
⇒Europe
1500s-Present

Glass beads
Europe 1800s-Present
⇒South Africa

Distribution of Beads and Bead
Materials in Africa

Reference: Lois Sherr Dubin, *The History of Beads: From 30,000 B.C. to
the Present*, Harry N. Abrams, 1987

Natural Material Beads

The oldest beads are believed to have been made from readily available materials such as shells and ostrich eggs.

Among shells, it is the cowrie that is most widely used for decoration, both past and present. They were used to decorate ceremonial masks because they were believed to possess magical powers. The Hausa tribe adorned their wedding ornaments with cowrie shells, and various ethnic groups like the Yoruba, Dogon, Maasai, and Senufo used them in their rituals. Cowrie shells are featured on a Kuba mask found on p. 24, but you will also find them used extensively in other photos throughout the book as decorations.

Bones, teeth, and claws symbolized protection, good fortune, power, and prosperity and were believed to transfer these qualities to those who wore them, thus shielding them from evil forces. Teeth from powerful predators like lions and leopards were worn by chiefs and diviners to enhance their magical abilities. Snake vertebrae were thought to ward off snake bites, while ivory was associated with status and wealth. The meaning of most such materials varied depending on the type of animal they came from.

Stones were readily available in the natural environment and were one of the earliest materials used for bead-making. Stone beads such as amazonite, crystal, agate, carnelian, granite, jasper, and bauxite have been produced and widely traded in Africa for centuries. Many of the stone beads excavated around the ancient cities of Djenné and Timbuktu, for example, traveled to Africa through trade routes spanning the Sahara Desert and were even brought from distant regions like India and China.

The natural materials used for beads had their own significance. African people believed that by wearing these beads, they could enhance their power, courage, and magic; ward off negative energy; and bring peace to their families. The belief in the power of natural materials, which has existed for centuries, continues in parts of Africa to this day.

MUKENGA

This is a helmet mask of the Kuba tribe. It is decorated with cowrie shells and glass beads. It's a unique beadwork mask known as the Kuba Mukenga.

Kuba tribe
Democratic Republic of
the Congo

SLING BAG

This is a sling bag from the Kuba tribe of the Congo. It features a wooden container decorated with raffia fiber, cowrie shells, and glass beads.

Kuba tribe
Democratic Republic of the Congo

KHOMEISA

This is a necklace worn by the Tuareg nomadic people of the Sahara Desert in Mali. It is used not only by the Tuareg but also by the Berber and Sonrai tribes of Niger, Algeria, Morocco, and Mauritania.

It consists of leather adorned with shells, or ostrich eggshells. A cord decorated with glass beads is threaded through it. It serves as a talisman, similar to the "Hand of Fatima," which can also be found in Middle Eastern countries like Turkey.

Tuareg tribe
Mali

CONUS SHELL BEADS

Conus refers to a group of spiral shells belonging to the Conidae family.
Only the tip of the shell is used. Even today, women in northwestern Mali
and Mauritania use them as hair ornaments. Small shells are also sometimes
attached to amulets and bracelets. The smaller these carved beads are, the less
circulated and more preferred. That is why some old shells are newly carved, as
shown on the right page.

Size: L20 (¾ inch) ×
φ20 (¾ inch) (two
shells combined)

Suraka tribe, Tuareg tribe
Mauritania

CONUS SHELL BEADS

These carved shell beads are from Mauritania or Mali. The beads themselves are old, but the carvings are newly added.

Size: L42 (1⅝ inches) × φ49 (2 inches) (two shells combined)

Fulani tribe, Suraka tribe Mali

CONUS SHELL AND BIVALVE SHELL BEADS

These are thick, heavy shell beads. In the photo above, the bead at the center with a stripe pattern was made from old bivalve shells.

Size: L25 (1 inch) × W30 (1¼ inches) (striped pattern)

Suraka tribe
Mauritania

CONUS SHELL BEADS

Large conus shells are used here.

Size: L32 (1¼ inches) × φ45 (1¾ inches)

Dogon tribe
Mali

CONUS SHELL BEADS

These are extra-large conus shell beads. The largest is approximately 9 cm (3½ inches). These were used as protective charms, usually one or two, incorporated into pieces of jewelry. These shell beads are typically stored at the Beads Museum (Musée des Perles in Sévaré), Mopti region, Mali.

Size: L15.8 (⅝ inch) × φ91.2 (3⅝ inches)

Dogon tribe
Mali

COWRIE SHELL ADORNMENTS THAT SERVED AS CURRENCY

In Mali, cowrie shells are known as *kolon*. *Kolon* served as a form of trade currency. The cowrie shells shown above were used as currency. In addition, they have been widely used for divination in Africa. Since they come from the sea, they held even greater value in inland areas and were considered a secure investment. They were easily exchangeable for various goods at any time. Cowrie shells remain popular to this day.

Used by various tribes
Mali

This is a photo from a wedding. The bride's necklace, bracelet, and earrings are made of cowrie shells. Both bride and groom are dressed in garments with cowrie shell patterns.

YORUBA IVORY NECKLACE

This is a necklace made of ivory that was worn by ethnic groups like the Yoruba and Igbo in Nigeria.

Size: L12.4 (½ inch) ×
φ9.7 (⅜ inch)

Yoruba tribe
Nigeria

This ivory pipe decorated with glass beads features a carved human face adorned with cowrie shells. Collected in the Democratic Republic of the Congo.

COW BONE BEADS

These cow bone beads were obtained about 25 years ago. My uncle made them. Originally, my uncle was an antiques dealer, but he found that old cow bone beads would sell quite quickly, so he decided to make beads using new cow bones. He collected cow bones, cleaned them thoroughly, cut them into suitable sizes, polished them, and finally crafted them into necklaces like these. It was all done by hand.

Size: L22.6 (⅞ inch) × φ45 (1¾ inches)

Dogon tribe
Mali

HIPPO TEETH BEADS

These are striking hippo teeth beads, available in various parts of West Africa. They aren't actually made from hippopotamus teeth; they are made from shells, only obtaining the name "hippo teeth beads" because of their resemblance to hippopotamus teeth.

Size: L61.4 (2⅜ inches) × H43.8 (1¾ inches)

Yoruba tribe
Mali

Natural Material Beads

SA-KOLO

These beads are made from snake vertebrae, known as *Sa-Kolo* in Mali. Snake bone beads, passed down since ancient times, were believed to protect the wearer against snake bites and have been used as protective charms for centuries. The natural old vertebrae beads are quite scarce. The most common are snake bone beads (see photo below), which are famous as "Bohemian beads." Among the five strands, the outer four consist of natural old snake bone beads, while the inner strand consists of snake bone beads made of bronze.

Size: L13.5 (½ inch) × φ20.2 (¾ inch) (center of the outer strand)

These are Bohemian glass snake bone beads (for more details, see p. 214).

CORAL

Coral has long been considered a precious ornament, not just in Africa, but also in Japan, other parts of Asia, Europe, North America, and various other parts of the world. Even today, there are regions in Nigeria where elegant coral beads are worn for weddings. These beads have also been widely used in Arab countries, including Morocco. In Japan, they have been used in *kanzashi* hairpins. China is known to have a deep affection for coral and is said to collect the largest variety and quantity of coral in the world. Like other natural beads, coral is believed to possess protective properties.

BRANCH CORAL

In Western countries, it is called branch coral. Here we see small examples.

Size: L23 (⅞ inch) × φ3 (⅛ inch)

Bamanan tribe
Mali, Segou region

MOUNTAIN CORAL

These Nigerian mountain corals have many holes. Nigeria is the country in Africa with the most abundant variety and quantity of coral. They are indispensable beads in Nigeria's Edo (or Bini) culture, loved as adornments by royalty, nobility, and commoners alike.

Size: L25 (1 inch) × φ25 (1 inch)

Yoruba, Igbo
Nigeria

BRANCH CORAL

These are thicker branch coral obtained in Mali. In North African Islamic communities – such as Morocco – they are used in combination with silver, gold, and amber to make beautiful jewelry.

Size: L68 (2⅝ inches) × φ9 (⅜ inch)

Mali, Mopti region

EARTH

DJENNÉ-KOLO

Djenné-Kolo (a spindle) is a tool used by women in Djenné for spinning thread.
The *Djenné-Kolo* is attached to the end of a stick so that it can be smoothly and
quickly rotated. Originally, these weren't beads, but women in Djenné came to
use them as such. It is said that many of these beads were decorated or painted
to make the women's spinning work more enjoyable.

Size: L30 (1¼ inches) ×
φ30 (1¼ inches)

Mali, Mopti region

Size: L25 (1 inch) ×
φ20 (¾ inch)

Mali, Mopti region

These colorful contemporary terracotta beads were made not as spindles but as beads.

The famous mosque in Djenné, known as "The City of Mud."

Contemporary terracotta beads from Djenné, made to resemble a necklace similar to the one above.

FARA-KONON

Fara refers to stones, and *Konon* refers to beads. The two words together encompass beads made from various types of stones. *Fara-Konon* are crafted from natural stones found in the environment and made into jewelry. The history of these beads began with the belief that one could harness the power of natural elements – like stones, shells, wood, and bones – by shaping them into adornments. This concept remains unchanged to this day, as evidenced by our fascination with gemstones.

NATURAL STONE BEADS

These are exceptionally large beads crafted from nature's bounty. Some appear to have been naturally perforated. Later, they came to be valued for their size.

Size: φ98.2 (3⅞ inches)

Dogon tribe
Mali

NATURAL STONE DISK BEADS

These are disk-shaped beads obtained from the vicinity of Timbuktu, a city in the Sahara Desert of Mali. They are made from agate and granite.

Size: L38 (1½ inches) × φ75 (3 inches)

Dogon tribe
Mali

NATURAL STONE BEADS

These beads were obtained from the vicinity of Djenné. They are simple stones with holes drilled through them.

Size: L35 (13/8 inches) × φ50 (2 inches)

Mali, Djenné

NATURAL STONE BEADS

These beads were obtained in a Dogon tribe city near the famous Bandiagara Escarpment. These stones have multiple holes, allowing them to be worn by simply threading a cord through them.

Size: L23 (⅞ inch) × φ35 (1⅜ inches) (center right)

Dogon
Mali

FOSSIL BEADS

These fossil beads were excavated in the Sahara Desert in Mali and are believed to date back to the Neolithic era. Similar beads have also been unearthed in Niger and Mauritania.

Size: L23 (⅞ inch) × φ40 (1⅝ inches)

Mali, Gao region

47

FARA-KONON CRYSTAL BEADS

These are crystal stone beads excavated in Mali, specifically in the Timbuktu and Gao regions. They mostly take on a gentle bi-cone shape and are estimated to be over 3,000 years old.

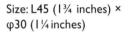

Size: L45 (1¾ inches) × φ30 (1¼ inches)

Mali, Timbuktu, Gao

FARA-KONON KURUKURUNI

These stone beads were unearthed around the Timbuktu and Gao regions. Despite being round, the holes aren't centered. Rather, they are closer to the edge. This results in an uneven string of beads. These smaller stone beads are referred to as *Kurukuruni*. They are relatively scarce, thus making them more valuable. They come in various materials, including crystal, agate, jasper, and others.

Size: L20 (¾ inch) × φ60 (2⅜ inches)

Mali, Timbuktu, Gao

FARA-KONON BARUKONI

These beads were mined around Gao. They come in bi-cone and tube shapes, and the name "Baruconi" is derived from the Bamanan word *Barucon*, meaning "cask" or "barrel." The stones are made of crystal, carnelian, granite, or bauxite, and come in various colors. Larger beads have limited circulation. They were once used by high-status individuals.

Size: L20 (¾ inch) × φ28 (1⅛ inches) (center-right)

Dogon
Mali

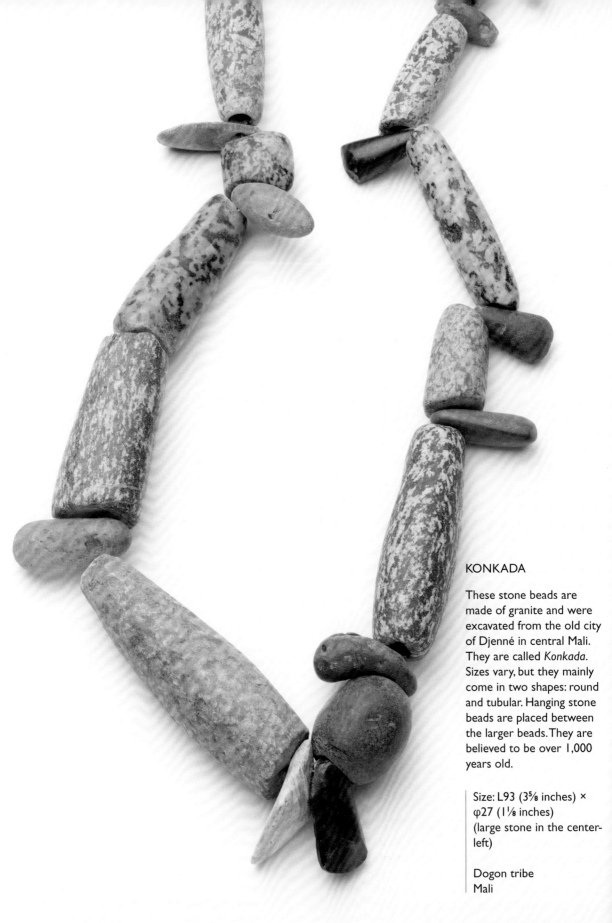

KONKADA

These stone beads are made of granite and were excavated from the old city of Djenné in central Mali. They are called *Konkada*. Sizes vary, but they mainly come in two shapes: round and tubular. Hanging stone beads are placed between the larger beads. They are believed to be over 1,000 years old.

Size: L93 (3⅝ inches) × φ27 (1⅛ inches) (large stone in the center-left)

Dogon tribe
Mali

KONKADA

There are extra-large, medium, and small *Konkada* beads. The small and medium sizes circulate widely, but the extra-large ones are relatively scarce. Those in good condition are among the true masterpieces of the Dogon.

Size: L148 (5⅞ inches) × φ30 (1¼ inches)

Dogon tribe
Mali

FARA-KONON AGATE BEADS

These are round agate beads. They come in various shapes and sizes. The one on the left represents the most common size, while the other is exceptionally large.

Size: L6 (¼ inch) × φ10 (⅜ inch) (left)
Size: L20 (¾ inch) × φ25 (1 inch) (right)

Mali

CUT AGATE BEADS

In Mali, the Dogon and Fulani tribes, as well as the Mossi tribe in Burkina Faso, cherish these cut agate beads. They are believed to have originated in India. The large bead in the center, obtained in Burkina Faso, is exceptionally rare. These cut beads have been collected gradually in Mali.

Size: L15 (⅝ inch) × φ50 (2 inches)

Fulani tribe
Mali, Burkina Faso

WHITE STRIPED AGATE

These are white agate beads with striped patterns. They are often heavy and have an impressive appearance. They are believed to have been produced in India (or Germany) in the early 19th century, with many of them being distributed through Nigeria. These examples were acquired in Mopti and are available in various parts of West Africa.

Size: L58 (2¼ inches) × φ23 (⅞ inch)

Mali, Mopti region

The colored beads in this inset photo are the stone beads.

FULANI

This is an amulet (talisman) worn by Fulani women living in Mali and Burkina Faso. The early versions of these amulets were made from stone beads, primarily using natural crystals and agate. During the colonial era, glass beads from Czechoslovakia became available. The photo above shows a mix of both types of beads, with the glass beads generally being smaller in size.

Size: L18 (¾ inch) × φ38 (1½ inches) (front-center white stone)

Fulani tribe
Mali

AMAZONITE

Amazonite varies slightly in shape and color depending on the region where it is mined. Colors range from light green to dark green and blue. Nigerian amazonite tends to produce large, teardrop-shaped beads. Serpentine and scorzalite are in a similar family to amazonite.

Size: L16 (⅝ inch) × φ24 (1 inch)

Mauritania

Large Amazonite from Nigeria.

New amazonite from around 1990, obtained in Mauritania.

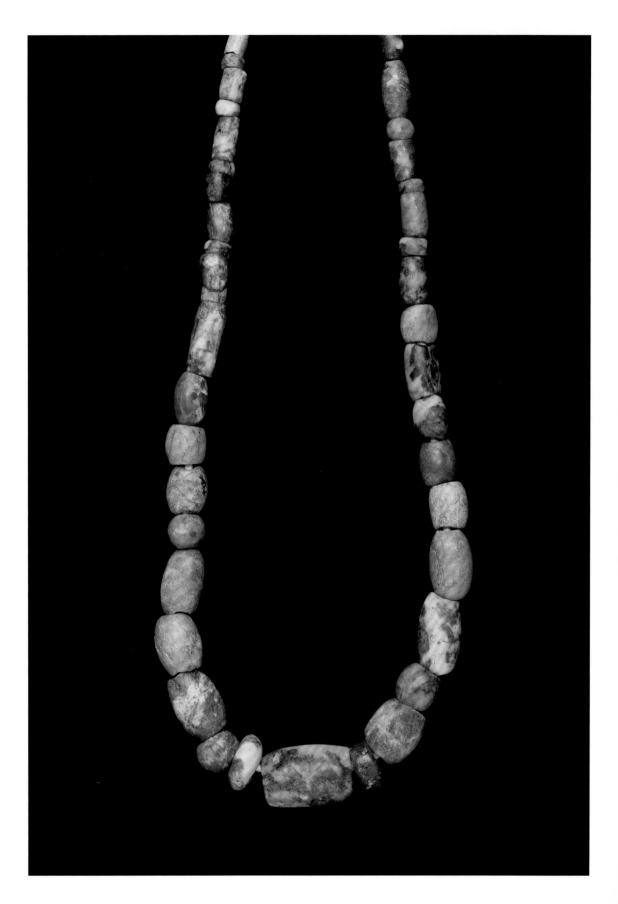

This is jewelry from local peoples. On the left are scorzalite and *Hamada* eye beads. On the right is amazonite with serpentine on each side. These pieces were obtained in the town of Nara near the border between Mali and Mauritania.

SCORZALITE

Scorzalite is a relatively rare variety of amazonite. Some people refer to amazonite, scorzalite, and serpentine collectively as amazonite. Scorzalite is less well-known, and many prefer to reserve the term amazonite specifically for true amazonite and serpentine. Scorzalite is typically blue or bluish-white. It took several years to collect these beads as they were acquired one-by-one.

Size: L28.9 (1¼ inches) × φ19.8 (¾ inch)

Mali, Mauritania, Sahara region

SERPENTINE

Serpentine is related to amazonite. It is softer than the typical light green amazonite and has a dark green color. The photo above shows large serpentine beads excavated from Nara, near the border between Mali and Mauritania.

Size: L55 (2⅛ inches) × φ28 (1⅛ inches)

Mali, Nara city

DOGON STONE BEADS

When I was in Mopti, I helped a dealer thread a large number of stone beads. There were probably 200 to 300 strands. From among those, I selected some beads to create this strand. They are very memorable beads.

Size: L13 (½ inch) × φ13 (½ inch)

Dogon tribe
Mali

BAUXITE

These are old stone beads made from bauxite obtained in Guinea. They come in various shapes, including round and tubular. Currently, Guinea boasts the highest bauxite production in Africa.

Size: L18 (¾ inch) × φ18 (¾ inch)

Guinea

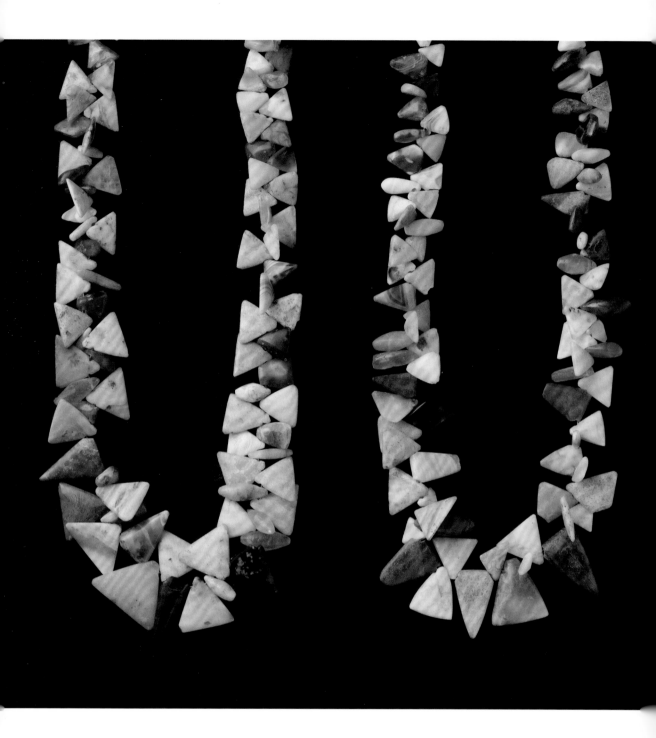

TRIANGLE BEADS

These are stone bead strands excavated around the old city of Djenné. They are rare triangular beads that were delicately crafted by the few skilled stone artisans of that time. Triangular beads were believed to possess protective energy and were made from crystal, agate, jasper, granite, etc. The method of drilling holes was different from today; they were drilled from both sides, which sometimes resulted in misaligned holes within the beads. Stones with beautiful patterns are particularly popular.

Size: L22.4 (⅞ inch) ×
H22.8 (⅞ inch) ×
D3.6 (⅛ inch)
(tinted white bead on
right of central red bead)

Mali, Sahara region

TRIANGLE BEADS

These are meticulously chosen double strands of triangle beads. On the left we find carnelian. On the right is white striped agate.

Size: L19.2 (¾ inch) × H19 (¾ inch) × D6.1 (¼ inch) (center bead on right strand)

Mali, Sahara region

DOG BONE BEADS

One of the least-distributed beads on the market is the dog bone bead. Although many are made of glass, their prototypes are made from natural stones such as crystal, granite, and agate, as shown in the photo. Dog bone beads are also called "Hourglass Beads" because of their hourglass-like shape. Glass-made dog bone beads are relatively common in melon bead strings (see p. 148).

Size: L37.4 (1½ inches) × φ21.5 (⅞ inch)

Dogon tribe
Mali

AMBER

Amber is fossilized resin from ancient pine and cedar trees. It has been prized as jewelry throughout the world. Amber is available in orange, yellow, red, black, and green. The rarest specimens are blue (found in Dominican Republic and Indonesia). Younger, semi-fossilized amber is called copal while heat-compressed, artificial amber is called ambroid. The overwhelming allure of amber means that there are many imitations made of synthetic resins and plastics (see p. 235).

Size: L26.2 (1 inch) × φ48.7 (1⅞ inches)

Fulani tribe
Mali

Amber beads joined with copper and nickel.

REPAIRED AMBER BEADS

These are repaired amber beads from the Suraka tribe. The Suraka people repair broken amber beads with metal, just as broken pottery is repaired with metal joints in Japan. The repaired beads are considered more beautiful and therefore more valuable. Fitting repair materials include silver, copper, bronze, and nickel. In some cases, unbroken amber – without any cracks or fissures whatsoever – is decorated as well. The Suraka people live in the Sahara Desert, mainly in Mauritania and the western part of Mali, where they herd goats. When most people think of the Suraka in Mali, goat meat is the first thing that comes to mind.

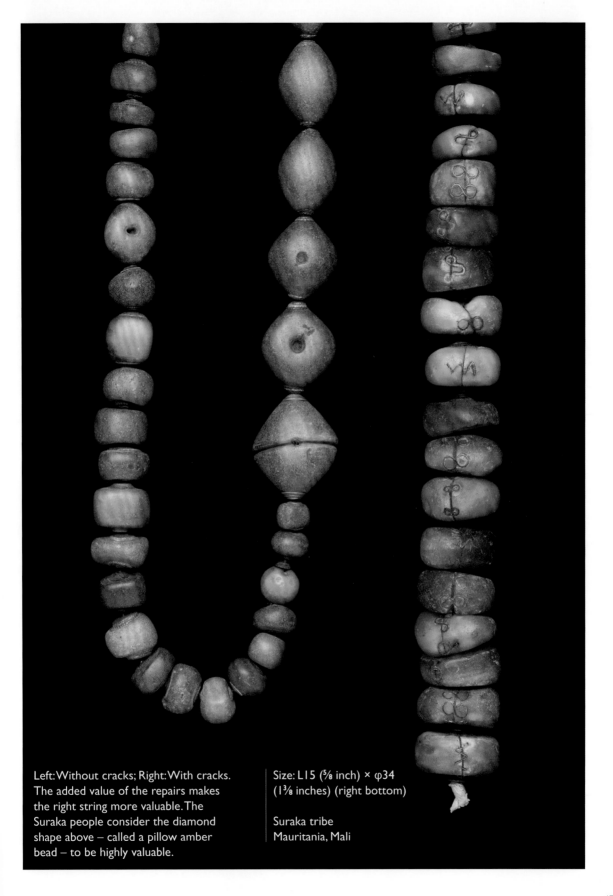

Left: Without cracks; Right: With cracks.
The added value of the repairs makes
the right string more valuable. The
Suraka people consider the diamond
shape above – called a pillow amber
bead – to be highly valuable.

Size: L15 (⅝ inch) × φ34
(1⅜ inches) (right bottom)

Suraka tribe
Mauritania, Mali

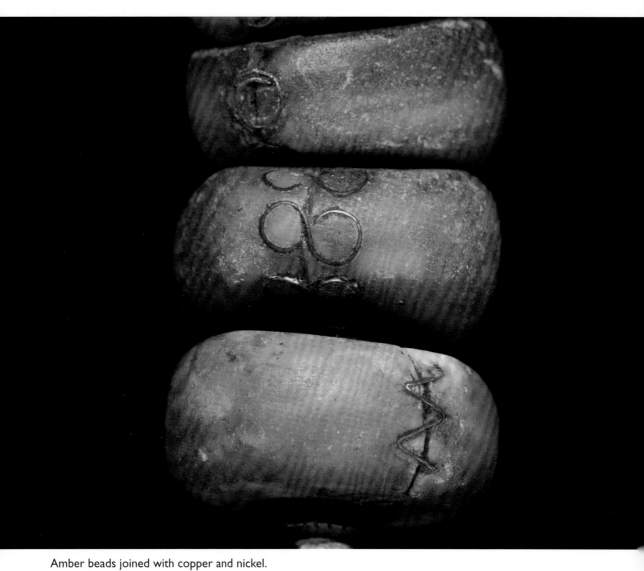

Amber beads joined with copper and nickel.

AMBER POWDER

People have believed in the mysterious powers of amber since ancient times. It is even used in modern medicine and is said to be beneficial for anti-aging. There are beauty benefits as well, and cosmetic products containing amber have now become popular. In the past, amber powder was said to be accessible only to the nobility. This powder was obtained in Mali and includes chunks that have not yet been fully ground into powder.

A woman wearing a Baltic amber necklace. Photo taken in Bamako, Mali.

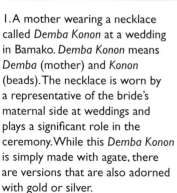

1. A mother wearing a necklace called *Demba Konon* at a wedding in Bamako. *Demba Konon* means *Demba* (mother) and *Konon* (beads). The necklace is worn by a representative of the bride's maternal side at weddings and plays a significant role in the ceremony. While this *Demba Konon* is simply made with agate, there are versions that are also adorned with gold or silver.

2. The bride's birthmother is the woman who isn't wearing a *Demba Konon*. The other three women are *Demba* and wearing *Demba Konon*. The woman on the right who wears the *Demba Konon* adorned with gold represents a *Demba* group in the wedding party. In Mali, during weddings, friends and relatives often wear outfits made from the same fabric. These four women are my sisters.

3. This *Demba* is wearing *Demba Konon* adorned with gold.

4. Now it's popular to drape a long *Konon* over one's shoulder.

5. A woman wearing *Demba Konon* at a wedding. She also has her *Konon* draped over her shoulder.

1. & 2. Women at a wedding wearing beads as hair ornaments, Fulani style.

3. Women wearing *Demba Konon* in the Fulani style at a wedding.

4. A man at a wedding wearing a traditional outfit and modern leather necklace.

1. Women dancing at a Dogon festival. They are wearing large copal necklaces and bracelets.

2. A festival venue in Mopti City. The woman's necklace is particularly eye-catching.

3. & 4. When I visited Congo in 2010, I went to a funeral. At the wake, people danced through the night while performing various rituals. No one cried or grieved. The attendees danced while wearing raffia, Kuba cloth costumes, cowrie shells and beads. On the right in photo 4 is the author of this book.

A young Fulani woman's hair ornaments. Fulani women usually wear a lot of beads like this as a fashion statement. The Fulani people were originally nomadic pastoralists, but now many of them have settled in Senegal, Nigeria, Kenya, and other parts of Africa. Therefore, they are called by various names: "Fula" in the Bamanan language. Other names include "Fulfulbe," "Peul," "Fulbe," "Pulaar," and "Fulbeere."

Trade Beads (1):
Trade with the Islamic World

In the Islamic world, there are several important regions when discussing glass art, such as Egypt, Mesopotamia, Syria, the Levant, and the Sassanian Persian Empire. Of particular significance as central hubs of bead manufacturing are Egypt, the Levant, and Syria.

The history of glass craftsmanship in Egypt dates back to ancient times, flourishing around the 14th century BCE. The invention of mosaic glass is attributed to Egyptian glass artisans, and by the 1st century BCE, it had become quite common. There was a significant glass bead center located in Fustat, near Cairo. During the 9th century to the 10th century, before the destruction of Fustat in 1168, the glass workshops of Fustat were particularly active in producing glass beads. Many of these beads were subsequently brought to West Africa.

In Africa, long-distance trade routes – including those across the Sahara and Indian Ocean – had already developed prior to the 15th century Age of Exploration. Islamic traders brought items from the Middle East, such as coral, cowrie shells, and glass beads, across to exchange them for West African goods like gold and ivory. Beads used in such trade are referred to as "trade beads."

Many of the beads discussed in this chapter were brought from Islamic regions – like Egypt – during what is known as the Islamic Golden Age. They were brought to thriving kingdoms that included the Ghana Empire, the Mali Empire, and the Songhai Empire. These beads have been unearthed in urban sites such as Gao, Timbuktu, and the trade hub of Djenné.

FAIENCE BEADS

These are Egyptian-made faience beads. Faience is a mixture of fired quartz and calcium carbonate with a glassy glazed coating. It has been produced since around 4100 BCE in Mesopotamia and Egypt. It was used as a substitute for turquoise and lapis lazuli in adornments and burial artifacts.

Size: L18 (¾ inch) × φ22 (⅞ inch)

Mali, Timbuktu

Size: L8 (¼ inch) ×
φ12 (½ inch)

Mali, Timbuktu

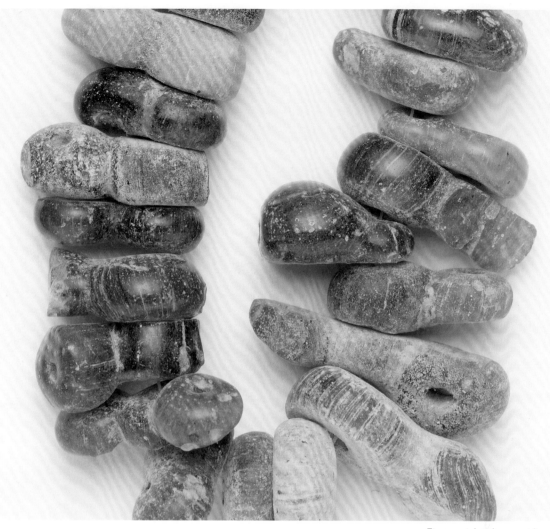

Figure-eight shape with two holes.

NILA BEADS

Nila beads are estimated to date back to around the 7th century. These glass beads were excavated from Gao, Mali, but they are still being discovered in the ancient towns of Djenné and Timbuktu. When unearthed, they are sometimes found alongside eye beads, metal jewelry, and pure gold jewelry. In addition to the popular blue color, they come in green, yellow, white, and gray. Particularly scarce and unique are the double-holed, figure-eight-shaped beads. Small-sized Nila beads are referred to as *Tasa* locally.

Size: L4.4 (1⁄8 inch) × φ18.1 (3⁄4 inch) (right)

Mali, Gao

Size: L4.5 (⅛ inch) ×
φ9.4 (⅜ inch) (right)

Mali, Gao

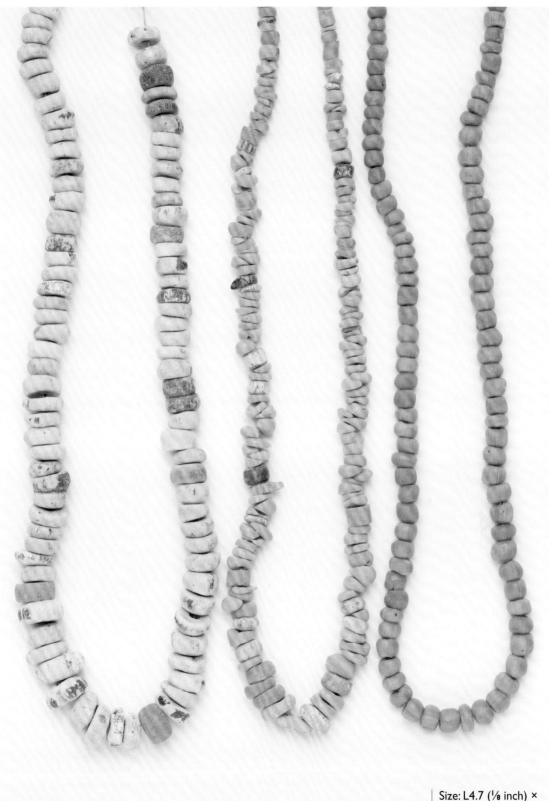

Size: L4.7 (⅛ inch) ×
φ10.4 (⅜ inch) (left)

Mali, Gao

KAMADA

These beads are said to date from around the 8th century to the 12th century. Among the Djenné eye beads (known as *Nyekirima ye* in the Bambara language), there are *Kamada* and *Hamada* eye beads. These are the *Kamada* type. Eye beads are thought to ward off evil spirits. Just as most European-made trade beads were not used in their country of production, eye beads were made in Egypt but found in highest demand in the Mali Kingdom of Djenné. There they fetched high prices and were often traded for luxury items like gold and silver.

Size: L14.9 (⅝ inch) × φ16.5 (⅝ inch)

Mali, Djenné

KAMADA

These are eye beads unearthed in the ancient town of Djenné. The passage of time and environmental changes have led to the loss of most of the clear eyes. Some people refer to *Kamada* as Islamic beads or Roman beads.

Size: L10 (⅜ inch) × φ13 (½ inch)

Mali, Djenné

KAMADA

These are rare inset blue eye beads. They are believed to have been produced in Fustat. Fustat was the former capital of Egypt before Cairo.

Size: L13.9 (½ inch) × φ16.1 (⅝ inch)

Mali, Djenné

The central bead has lost one of its eyes over time.

HAMADA

This is an eye bead that was unearthed in Djenné. It's called *Hamada* when the circles are doubled. Eye beads are also found in Mauritania. The bead above is smaller than the typical blue eye *Hamada*. There are eyes on both sides of the central line, similar to the *Kamada* on p. 82.

Size: L13 (½ inch)
× φ15.3 (⅝ inch)

Mali, Djenné

KAMADA, HAMADA

These beads were excavated from the ancient town of Djenné. While eye beads are typically round, this strand contains rare tubular beads that are still in excellent condition. These eye beads are said to ward off evil spirits like the famous Turkish evil eye beads.

Size: L20 (¾ inch)
× φ9 (⅜ inch)

Mali, Djenné

EYE BEADS

These are members of the blue eye beads excavated in Djenné. They are also called "eye beads" even though they are tubular beads with rare vertical and horizontal striped patterns and are scarce.

Size: L25 (1 inch)
× φ13 (½ inch) (left)

Mali, Djenné

EYELESS EYE BEADS

Excavated in Djenné, these beads have no eyes and in Mali they are called "eyeless eye beads." They were originally the same blue color as blue eye beads, but their color has faded to something resembling silver.

Size: L12 (½ inch)
× φ12 (½ inch)

Mali, Djenné

Traditional market held every Monday in front of the Great Mosque.

ANCIENT CITY OF DJENNÉ

Djenné was the most prosperous city south of the Sahara around the 7th century. Located in the Mopti region in central Mali, it is one of Mali's three major tourist destinations, alongside the Dogon region (including the Bandiagara Escarpment) and Timbuktu. It is the most popular tourist spot in West Africa.

When you think of Djenné, the image of the world's oldest and largest earthen mosque will likely come to mind. Excavation of Djenné-Djeno, which is part of old Djenné, has revealed structures dating back to the 3rd century BCE. Construction of the first colossal earthen building is believed to have begun in the 13th century when Mali began its conversion to Islam. Subsequently, empires such as the Songhai, Bamanan, Morocco, and Massina tried to exert control over Timbuktu and Djenné. The mosque has been destroyed and rebuilt several times as different rulers came to power. It was last reconstructed in 1907 and stands to this day as it was then.

The mosque is about 20 meters high and can accommodate around 3,000 people. It features a unique architectural style that combines Islamic and Sudanese elements. Every year, there is a day dedicated to repainting the mosque's walls. This day brings tourists from all over the world to Djenné and its surroundings. Additionally, Djenné market takes place in front of the mosque every Monday, which creates a truly festive atmosphere.

Most buildings in Djenné are constructed with earth. The majority of residential homes around the mosque are two stories tall. Due to the absence of earthquakes, these structures can last for several centuries with regular maintenance.

Clay found in Djenné is high in quality and thus valued the world over for its use in pottery, terracotta figurines, and sculptures. Djenné-Djeno terracotta, in particular, trades at high prices. During Djenné's heyday, luxury items like eye beads were brought to the city from various parts of the world.

EYE BEAD

This is a rare Djenné eye bead with striking yellow eyes.

Size: L9.5 (⅜ inch) × φ11.3 (½ inch)

Mali, Djenné

EYE BEAD

This eye bead was excavated in Djenné and combines transparent blue with red and yellow eyes.

Size: L9.7 (⅜ inch) × φ10.4 (⅜ inch)

Mali, Gao

EYE BEAD

This eye bead was excavated in Djenné.

Size: L11.1 (½ inch) × φ11.3 (½ inch)

Mali, Djenné

MOSAIC EYE BEAD

This multi-colored mosaic eye bead was excavated in Djenné.

Size: L13.7 (½ inch) × φ9 (⅜ inch)

Mali, Djenné

FAKURUN

These are beads known as *Fakurun*, meaning "turtle shell." Shown above is a single strand of beads with purple turtle shell patterns. Some people call them *Morfia*. These beads were excavated in the desert town of Timbuktu in Mali. While the basic color is purple, rare blue variations also exist. Beads with turtle shell patterns are the hallmark of the highest-quality beads.

Size: L17.2 (⅝ inch)
× φ12.9 (½ inch)

Mali, Timbuktu

FAKURUN

This is a beautiful purple *Fakurun* bead with turtle shell patterns.

Size: L12.3 (½ inch) × φ12.5 (½ inch)

Mali, Sahara region

FAKURUN

Unique mosaic eye beads in a monochromatic shade of purple.

Size: L17 (⅝ inch) × φ11 (½ inch) (left)
Size: L11 (½ inch) × φ8 (¼ inch) (right)

Mali, Gao region

MORFIA EYE BEAD

This is a good-condition *Morfia* eye bead with a feather-like pattern, dating back to around the 10th century. In the northern Malian village of Takamba, a large number of ancient beads like this have been discovered. In the past, people in Mauritania and the northern regions of Mali believed that these beads possessed magical and healing powers.

Size: L16 (⅝ inch) ×
φ16 (⅝ inch)

Mali, Takamba village

Broken *Morfia* beads

MORFIA

This is a *Morfia* bead excavated from the vicinity of Gao, Mali. It is estimated to date back to the 10th century. While this particular bead is Islamic, similar examples have been found in Europe as well. It resembles Javanese beads known as Manik Pelangi. *Morfia* are also known as rainbow beads.

Size: L17 (⅝ inch) × φ18 (¾ inch)

Mali, Gao

MORFIA

These beads were excavated in Honbori Village in the Mopti region of Mali. They are a rare type of eye bead with multiple eyes that are relatively large. In the local area, they are referred to as *Fakurun* or *Morfia*. The name *Fakurun* derives from the turtle shell pattern.

Size: L16 (⅝ inch) × φ19 (¾ inch) (right)

Mali, Gao

FEATHER BEAD

This is a long tube-shaped monochrome feather bead from the Roman period.

Size: L36.9 (1½ inches) × φ11.3 (½ inch)

Mali, Sahara region

FEATHER BEADS

This is one strand of two different monochrome feather beads from the Roman period.

Size: L15 (⅝ inch) × φ10 (⅜ inch)

Mali, Gao

FEATHER BEAD

This is a monochrome round bead with feather-like patterns from the Roman period. The name comes from the feather-like pattern.

Size: L13 (½ inch) × φ15 (⅝ inch)

Mali, Sahara region

Similarly, this is a Roman period tubular, blue and black feather bead

FEATHER BEAD

This is a feather bead from the Islamic Golden Age. Among trade beads from the 18th and 19th centuries, feather beads are quite common. This is one of the original types of feather-patterned beads.

Size: L17 (⅝ inch) × φ11 (½ inch)

Mali, Sahara region

MOSAIC TAPESTRY BEADS

Locally, these beads are called "tapestry beads" because of their patterns, which resemble carpets. They are trade beads commonly found in the Mediterranean region. These beads come in both tubular and spherical forms.

Size: L14.5 (⅝ inch) × φ11.6 (½ inch) (right)

Mali, Gao

MOSAIC BEAD, TAPESTRY BEAD

On the left is an eye bead with mosaic patterns. On the right is a spherical tapestry bead.

Size: L7.5 (¼ inch) × φ10.7 (⅜ inch) (left)
Size: L10.9 (⅜ inch) × φ11.8 (½ inch) (right)

Mali, Gao

MOSAIC BEADS

These are tubular beads with radial patterns. They are rare, green-based mosaic beads excavated from Takamba village in Mali.

Size: L12 (½ inch) × φ8.6 (⅜ inch) (left)

Mali, Gao

MOSAIC BEADS

The bead on the left is a teardrop-shaped bead with vertical lines and intersecting stripes on a yellow base. I have never seen anything quite like it before.

On the bead on the right there are white, blue, and brown stripes on both sides of the centerline.

Size: L19.1 (¾ inch) × H10.6 (⅜ inch) × D8.1 (¼ inch) (left)
Size: L19.2 (¾ inch) × φ10.5 (⅜ inch) (right)

Mali, Gao

MOSAIC BEADS

These are tubular mosaic eye beads excavated in Mali. Similar beads have been found in the Middle East. Beads of this type have countless patterns.

Top left
Size: L16 (⅝ inch) × φ6 (¼ inch)

Mali, Gao region

Top right
Size: L16 (⅝ inch) × φ7 (¼ inch)

Mali, Sahara region

Bottom
Size: L12.6 (½ inch) × φ8.4 (⅜ inch) (right)

Mali, Gao

TURQUOISE EYE BEADS

These are beads with a turquoise base and mosaic eyes. They were excavated in Timbuktu in the Sahara Desert of Mali.

Size: L16.2 (⅝ inch) ×
H10.8 (⅜ inch) ×
D7.2 (¼ inch) (left)
Size: L8.4 (⅜ inch) ×
φ9.4 (⅜ inch) (right)

Mali, Timbuktu

MOSAIC WAVE PATTERN BEAD

This bead resembles an ancient Phoenician head pendant. It has a mosaic wave pattern and a vertical hole as well. This suggests the possibility of later attaching a fitting to the green portion in order to create a pendant.

Size: L18 (¾ inch) ×
φ11 (½ inch)

Mali, Sahara region

MOSAIC BEAD

This pendant bead, excavated in Djenné, has multiple concentric mosaic patterns affixed in a flat manner.

Size: L19.2(¾ inch) × H25.2 (1 inch) × D4.2 (⅛ inch)

Mali, Djenné

MOSAIC BEADS

These flat beads, excavated in Djenné, have multiple radial concentric mosaic patterns and feather-like patterns.

Size: L18.5 (¾ inch) × H26.2 (1 inch) × D3.8 (⅛ inch) (left front)

Mali, Djenné

TWISTED BEADS

The three beads on the left have monochrome spiral patterns (twisted beads). The one on the right is a pendant top-style bead.

Size: L10. 5 (⅜ inch) × H8 (¼ inch) × D3. 2 (⅛ inch) (second from right)

Mali, Sahara region

DOT BEADS

These are flat dot beads. They are said to be the prototype of European-made dot beads.

Size: L19 (¾ inch) × H22 (⅞ inch) (left)

Mali

EYE BEAD

This is an eye bead excavated from Djenné.

Size: L11 (½ inch) × φ19 (¾ inch)

Mali, Djenné

EYE BEAD

This is an eye bead excavated in Mali. It resembles the Warring States Period *Zhongtie Yanyu* (double-layered glass eye) bead excavated in Luoyang, China. Believed to be circa 1000 BCE.

Size: L11.8 (½ inch) × φ17.4 (¾ inch)

Mali, Sahara region

The bead in the middle is severely deteriorated.

EYE BEAD

This is a *Zhongtie Yanyu* (double-layered glass eye) bead excavated in Mali. It closely resembles Chinese-made beads from the Warring States period and is in excellent condition.

Size: L7 (¼ inch) × φ9 (⅜ inch)

Mali

MOSAIC EYE BEAD

This mosaic eye bead has a metal fitting attached and was excavated in Mali. While it doesn't have cracks, the effort taken to attach a metal fitting likely adds value. This technique is similar to that of pillow amber beads (see p. 66).

Size: L13.3 (½ inch) × φ15.6 (⅝ inch)

Mali, Gao

FACE BEAD

This trade bead is known as a "face bead." While Phoenician face beads are famous for their age, there are many other face beads. Actually, there are both "head beads" and "face beads." Simply put, for "head beads" the bead itself is shaped like a face, while "face beads" have faces drawn on the bead.

Size: L6.5 (¼ inch) × φ9.1 (⅜ inch)

Mali, Mopti region

EYE BEAD

This is an eye bead with white lines and radially drawn mosaic eyes.

Size: L8.7
(⅜ inch) ×
φ12.7 (½ inch)

Mali, Gao

WAVE PATTERN BEAD

This is an atypical wave patterned bead. In addition to the bead hole, there is another hole in the center that doesn't go all the way through.

Size: L9.5
(⅜ inch) ×
φ11.3 (½ inch)

Mali, Djenné

GAMING BEAD

Gaming beads were used as game pieces. In addition to this spiral pattern gaming bead, there are also dot beads. They come in various shapes, like dome-shaped or triangular. The term "gaming beads" only became popular in modern times.

Size: L12.9 (½ inch) ×
φ19 (¾ inch)

Mali, Sahara region

HEBRON BEADS

Hebron is an ancient city located in Palestine. It is considered a sacred site in Islam, Christianity, and Judaism. There are theories suggesting that these beads were either traded from Hebron to West Africa or produced in Sudan. Hebron beads have been particularly favored by people in the vicinity of Nigeria, where many of them have been excavated. They can also be found in Sudan, Mauritania, and other regions. Hebron beads are sometimes referred to as "Kano Beads," for Kano state in Nigeria.

Size: L17 (⅝ inch) × φ20 (¾ inch)

Nigeria, Kano state

Trade Beads (2):
Trade with Europe

During the 15th century Age of Exploration, European colonial powers expanded their influence in Africa. Towards the end of this era, the coastal peoples of West Africa began trading with Europeans. Portuguese explorers initiated the trade, but over the next 400 hundred years they were followed by Dutch, English, French, Belgian, and German traders. They brought glass beads to Africa from Venice, the Netherlands, and Czechoslovakia and exchanged them for African goods such as ivory, gold, copper, spices, and palm oil.

Exquisite glass beads with exotic shapes, intricate patterns, and vibrant colors were highly prized by Africans seeking both luxury and rarity. Traditional African beads had been crafted from natural materials such as shells, bones, teeth, ivory, and stones. European nations took note of the particular colors and patterns that were most popular and created a huge variety of beads to satisfy the varied preferences of each country and village. As a result, even commoners, who previously had no access to glass beads, were able to obtain them and wear them.

For African people, exotic and alluring foreign-made glass beads were considered symbols of wealth and status. They were treasured as family heirlooms and subsequently passed down through generations. Certain beads were highly prized and could only be used by kings and their courts. They became an integral part of African society.

In this chapter, we will focus on beads that were particularly prevalent in West Africa and were manufactured in places like Venice, the Netherlands, and Czechoslovakia.

ORIGINAL NECKLACES

These are necklaces worn by Fulani women living in the Mopti region of Mali.
On the left, we see a necklace made from natural ancient crystal beads, Djenné
beads, white hearts, and a six-layer chevron.

On the right, there is an original necklace made of Venetian beads called
Tiatiatio, millefiori, flower beads, green melon beads, and white hearts.

Fulani tribe
Mali, Mopti region

ORIGINAL NECKLACES

On the left is an ornament made with small beads from the indigenous Dogon people. Between the medium-sized colored and smaller dark green beads, you will find the larger Bohemian Baya beads. This accessory is likely a waist ornament made of love beads.

On the right, we find jewelry of the Fulani tribe from the Mopti region in Mali. This necklace combines natural ancient crystal stone beads, Djenné beads, white hearts, and flower beads.

Left:
Dogon tribe
Mali

Right:
Fulani tribe
Mali, Mopti region

MAASAI TRIBE NECKLACE

Above is a necklace worn by Maasai women. The Maasai tribe is well-known for its unique use of color. In Maasai society, roles and positions vary by gender and age. Males are categorized as "boys" from birth until around 20 years old, prior to undergoing circumcision. Then, they become "warriors" (*Moran*) until marriage, after which they are referred to as "elders." During the *Moran* phase, men adorn themselves extravagantly with beads. On the other hand, women wear beads throughout their lives. Wearing large and ornate necklaces is characteristic of *Ntito* (unmarried daughters). However, once they marry and become *Tomononi* they wear the earrings and other jewelry of married women. As such, observing bead decorations can help to easily distinguish whether someone is a boy, a warrior, or an elder. One can also distinguish whether a woman is unmarried or married.

Maasai tribe
Kenya

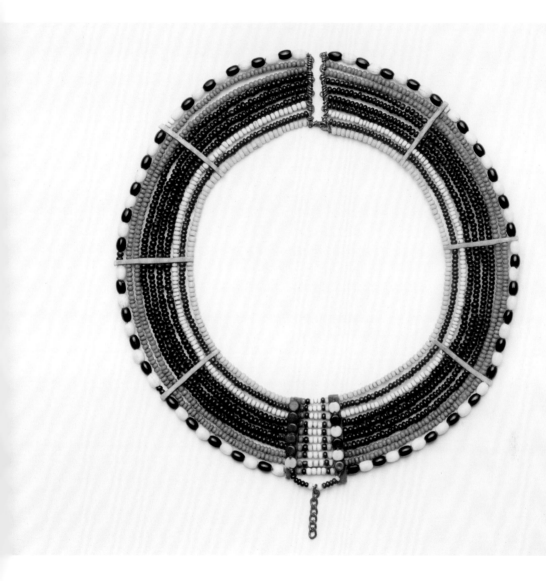

Central Kenya, Maasai
women

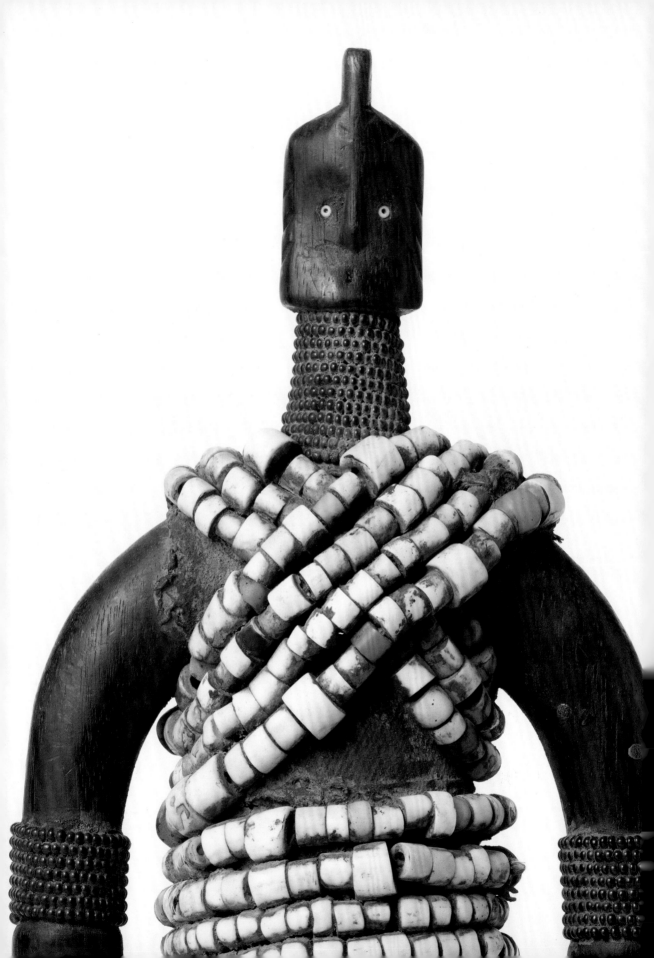

NAMJI DOLL

This is a doll from the
Namji tribe in Cameroon.
It is presented to brides
during marriage ceremonies
and is believed to bring
about safe childbirth and
the prosperity of any
offspring. The beads that
wrap around the body
of each doll vary, but the
Namji doll in the photo is
adorned with Bohemian
Baya beads.

Namji tribe
Cameroon

BEADWORK BAG

This is a beadwork bag from the Yoruba tribe of Nigeria. Similar items can also be found in Cameroon.

Yoruba tribe
Nigeria

BEAD AND COWRIE SHELL BELT

This is a raffia-made belt of the Kuba tribe from the Democratic Republic of Congo. The belt is decorated with cowrie shells and Baya beads, which are popular across Africa.

Kuba tribe
Democratic Republic of
Congo

A Kuba tribe woman wearing raffia clothing while adorned with headgear, several necklaces, and belts, all decorated with cowrie shells and glass beads.

BEADWORK SASH

This is a beadwork sash
from the Yoruba tribe in
Nigeria. It's a belt worn
on ceremonial occasions,
beautifully decorated with
beads and cowrie shells
in a vivid crocodile motif.
In some African regions,
crocodiles are revered as
tribal guardian spirits and
symbols of nobility/royalty.
Similar beadwork belts can
also be found in Cameroon.

Yoruba tribe
Nigeria

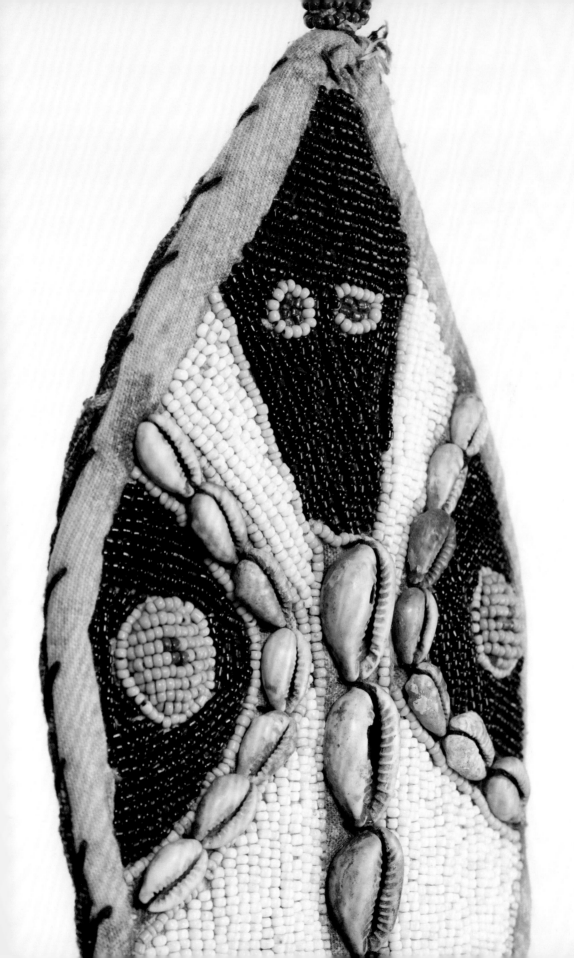

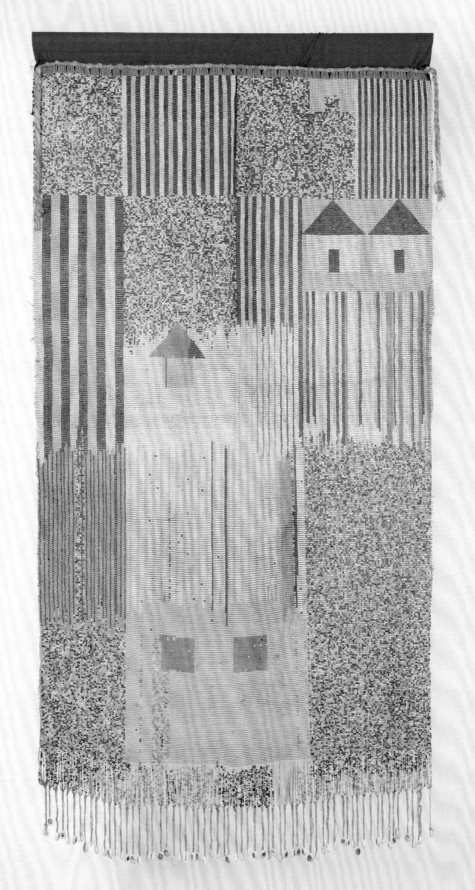

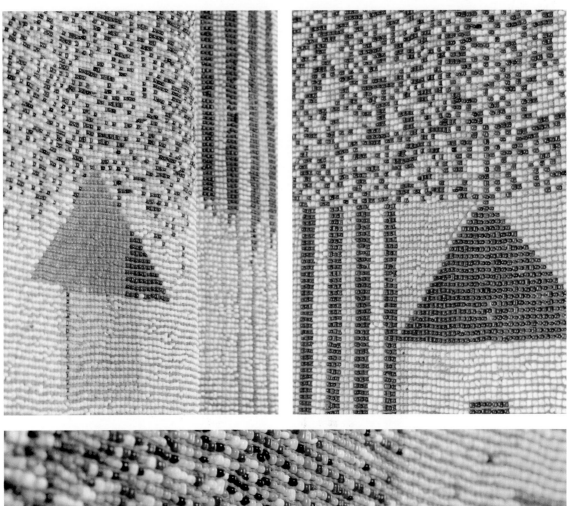

BEADWORK CURTAIN

These intricate beadwork pieces are from Cameroon, a country with people who have a long tradition of using beadwork – including ceremonial masks, clothing, stools, and more – throughout their daily lives. These particular pieces appear to be large beadwork decorations that resemble a curtain. They are made entirely from beads and cowrie shells. In addition, Cameroon is known for the beadwork of the Kirdi people, including short, beaded loincloths known as *Cache-sexe*.

| Cameroon

BEADWORK COSTUME

This is an old costume featuring unique motifs of birds and houses. It is made from both beads and cowrie shells.

Cameroon

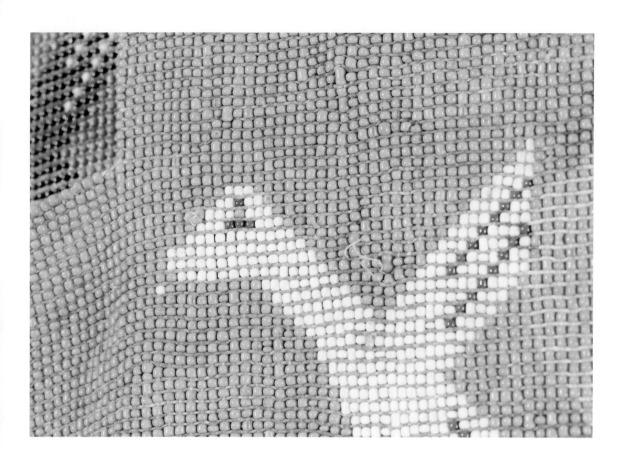

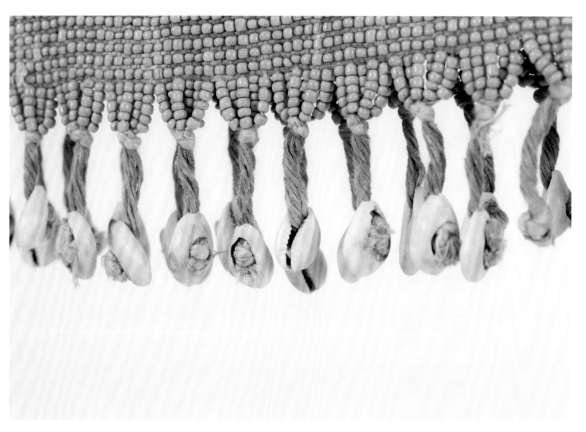

Venetian Glass Beads

The exact origins of glass production in Venice are not clear, but archaeological finds on the island of Torcello, a central hub in ancient Venice, have revealed glass furnaces, container fragments, and mosaic cubes that date from around 600 BCE. Glassmaking was also practiced in monasteries as early as the 8th century.

Bead production and exportation, both vital industries for Venice, can be traced back to the early 1300s. Venetian galleys transported beads to the Black Sea, Flanders, and England.

In 1291, the Venetian government took action to protect the glassmaking industry by relocating all glassworkers and their families to the island of Murano. There were strict penalties, including death, for those attempting to escape or reveal trade secrets. As a result, glass production and bead production flourished on Murano.

Over 100,000 different types and designs of beads were produced on Murano Island. Bead makers drew heavily on the intricate glass craftsmanship of ancient Egypt and Rome. Venetian glass craftsmanship reached its zenith during the Renaissance. While Venice nearly monopolized the bead market until the 18th century, the emergence of bead industries in Bohemia, Moravia, and the Netherlands – with the help of Venetian immigrant artisans – led to the gradual decline of Venetian glass bead production.

Intricate and ornate Venetian beads that captivated people in Africa, such as the *Tiatiatio*, continue to captivate the hearts of those who behold them even today.

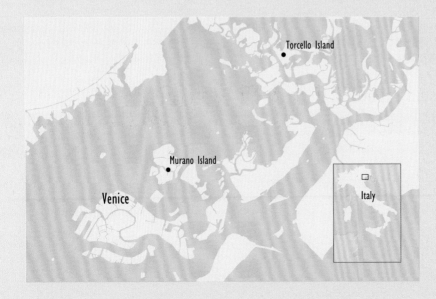

Torcello Island

Murano Island

Venice

Italy

CHEVRON

If we were to compare trade beads to the animal kingdom, chevron beads would be considered lions. There are very few collectors who don't appreciate chevron beads. In Italy, they are called rosetta beads, possibly because of their association with the Ancient Egyptian city of Rosetta. The story goes that around the 15th century, seven-layer rosetta beads, handmade in the Nile Delta's Rosetta, were brought to Italy. These served as the basis for mass production in Venice, eventually leading to the popularity of chevron beads.

In West Africa, my homeland, chevron beads go by various names depending on the region. Some regions refer to them as *Tie-konon* or *Issafall*. In Mali, the Bamanan people classify them as male chevron and female chevron. The male chevron is egg-shaped, while the female chevron is tube-shaped. In Mali, mini chevron beads are incorporated into jewelry, such as bracelets or waist ornaments, to serve as good luck charms for babies.

Chevron beads are also known as "star beads" because of their shape. Chevron beads originally came in 12 layers, but there are variations with five layers, eight layers, or modern designs with 16 or 18 layers.

Among the vast array of trade beads, the category encompassing chevron beads is most diverse. Sizes range from large (around 80 mm/3⅛ inches) to small (around 2–3 mm/⅛ inch). They usually have six layers, but there are variations with anywhere from two to 10 layers. Colors are mainly based on blue, with variations in white, red, yellow, green, and black, and there are even mosaics. Shapes can vary from egg-shaped to tube-shaped, dog bone, cone-shaped, and more.

Now, let me share a story I heard from my grandfather. In the past, many beads played a crucial role in trade with indigenous people worldwide. European countries brought guns, gunpowder, fabrics, and glass beads to trade with African and American indigenous populations. These goods were exchanged for ivory, gold, fur, wood, palm oil, and more. Slavery was indeed part of the exchange, but the fact is there was no exchange of slaves for chevron beads. There is a famous story of Christopher Columbus arriving in America, mistakenly thinking he had reached India, and presenting chevron beads to the indigenous people.

My grandfather had a business called a *Marabaka*, which is similar to what we now call an antique shop. When I was in school, I often visited him during work hours. He had served in the war, so he could speak French. One day, some Europeans were asking him various questions. After answering all their questions, my grandfather said, "I will tell you something that you didn't ask me about. In Farafina (Africa), there has never been an exchange of humans for trade beads."

A typical set of chevron beads. For more details, please refer to the next page.

The glass layers are cut to create a mountain (star-shaped) pattern. The pattern's shape and number of points changes depending on the cut. "Chevron" refers to a mountain-shaped pattern, and this term applies not only to beads but to any item with this particular pattern.

All the standard chevron patterns are encapsulated in these two beads. The Bamanan people separate the beads into female, tube-shaped, and male, egg-shaped. In general, tube-shaped beads are slightly smaller than egg-shaped ones. Both beads together are generally considered to be one pair of chevron beads.

Size: L30 (1¼ inches) × φ22 (⅞ inch) (left)
Size: L50 (2 inches) × φ30 (1¼ inches) (right)

Bamanan tribe
Mali, Segou region

GENESIS CHEVRON (ON THE RIGHT PAGE)

The genesis chevron refers to antique seven-layer chevron beads, the predecessor to mainstream six-layer chevron beads. It is widely believed that genesis chevrons originated in Egypt, although there are claims of Italian origin. The Italian term for the bead, "rosetta," might derive its name from the town of Rosetta in the Nile Delta, Egypt.

In 1496, the term "rosetta" was first documented in the records of an Italian glassworker named Angelo Barovier. His daughter, Marietta or Mari Barovier, is credited with naming the bead rosetta. It is believed that chevron beads existed in Egypt over 100 years before chevrons were produced in Venice.

Size: L42.7 (1⅝ inches) × φ30.6 (1¼ inches)

Mali, Burkina Faso, Nigeria, and other areas

HEXAGONAL CHEVRONS

These are rare hexagonally cut four-layer chevron beads with a silvered finish. Chevrons are also known as *Tie-konon* in West Africa among Bamanan people, or *Issafall* in Mali and Senegal.

Size: L32 (1¼ inches) × φ13 (½ inch)

Côte d'Ivoire, Abidjan

Typical chevron beads | Size: L42 (1⅝ inches) × φ32 (1¼ inches)

Bamanan tribe
Mali

HOW TO COUNT THE LAYERS OF CHEVRON BEADS

The way to count the layers of a standard six-layer chevron bead is from the white in the center hole to the blue on the surface. These beads consist of white, blue, white, red, white, blue, totaling six layers. There are three white layers, two blue layers, and one red layer.

For a seven-layer chevron bead, counting the layers is the same as for the six-layer version, but there is an additional blue layer inside the central white layer. So, there are three blue layers, three white layers, and one red layer. The layers can be difficult to see depending on the bead's condition, but in a seven-layer chevron, the core is blue.

A seven-layer chevron. The center is blue.

CUT CHEVRONS

On the left, there is a very large six-layer, four-sided cut chevron bead. In the center, you can see a flat four-sided cut chevron, and on the right is a diagonally cut chevron.

Size: L45 (1¾ inches) × φ29 (1¼ inches) (left)
Size: L38 (1½ inches) × φ17 (⅝ inches) (middle)
Size: L39 (1½ inches) × φ18 (¾ inches) (right)

Bamanan tribe
Mali

CUT CHEVRON

This is a beautiful blue six-layer, three-sided cut chevron.

Size: L27 (1⅛ inches) × φ24 (1 inch)

Bamanan tribe
Mali

DOG BONE CHEVRONS

These are rare six-sided dog bone chevron beads. They were obtained from the Segou region, where many Bamanan people reside. Among chevrons, this type of *Tie-konon* is highly esteemed and favored. They are scarce and thus possess high market value.

Size: L25 (1 inch) × φ26 (1 inch) (left)
Size: L28 (1⅛ inches) × φ20 (¾ inches) (right)

Bamanan tribe
Mali

CHEVRONS

These are rare six-layer, four-sided cut chevron beads. All three beads have interesting rear-facing cuts that give the appearance of being "twisted." They are quite hard to find.

Size: L33 (1¼ inches) × φ22 (⅞ inch) (left)

Bamanan tribe
Mali

SEVEN-LAYER STANDARD CHEVRON

This is a rare standard chevron bead. Although it has seven layers like a genesis chevron, it's actually a colonial-era Venetian chevron.

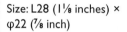

Size: L28 (1⅛ inches) × φ22 (⅞ inch)

Bamanan tribe
Mali

CHEVRON

This is a rare chevron with four layers. It features a blue chevron with green patterns. It was obtained in Nigeria.

Size: L26 (1 inch) × φ17 (⅝ inch)

Nigeria

GREEN CHEVRON

Green chevron beads are considered rare and hold a higher status than the standard blue chevrons. Note that there are seven-layer green chevrons as well. The way to count the layers is the same as for blue chevrons. The only difference is that the blue layers are replaced with green, and from the inside, it goes white, green, white, red, white, green.

The two in the front are egg-shaped males, while the rest are tube-shaped females. All five of them have six layers, but the leftmost yellow is rare. In this bead, the sequence is white, yellow, white, red, white, green. The green chevron with yellow was obtained in Nigeria, the rest are from Mali.

Size: L23 (⅞ inch) × φ17 (⅝ inch) (left)

Mali, Nigeria

BROKEN CHEVRON
This is the cross-section of a broken chevron bead. Whether antique or contemporary, the depth of patterns on the surface of beads is an indicator of advanced craftsmanship. Deeper patterns are less likely to fade over time.

BLACK CHEVRON

Two six-layer black chevron beads obtained in the city of Nara, Mali.

Size: L26 (1 inch) ×
φ20 (¾ inch) (left)

Bamanan tribe
Mali

YELLOW CHEVRON

Among the six-layer chevrons, these have fewer colors. They feature a standard six-layer chevron with red replaced by yellow. The layers are in the order of white, blue, white, yellow, white, blue.

Size: L26 (1 inch) ×
φ22 (⅞ inch) (center)

Nigeria

SEVEN-LAYER CHEVRON AND MODERN CHEVRON

On the left is an antique seven-layer chevron in brown, belonging to the Bamanan tribe. On the right, we have a red-based four-sided concave chevron from the 1990s.

Size: L26 (1 inch) × φ23 (⅞ inch) (left)
Size: L35 (1⅜ inches) × φ17 (⅝ inch) (right)

Bamanan tribe
Mali

FIVE-LAYER CHEVRON

Obtained in the city of Kolokani in the Kouloukoro region of Mali, this chevron is based on the one in the upper left photo. It is believed to have been made in the 18th century. It features a red base with horizontal lines in three colors: red, white, and blue.

Size: L33 (1¼ inches) × φ24 (1 inch) (left)

Bamanan tribe
Mali, Kouloukoro region

This is a slightly weathered chevron in red and white. Unlike the standard chevron, the pattern does not extend into the deeper parts of the bead.

COLLECTIBLE CHEVRONS

These are scarce collectible beads. If you look closely, you'll notice that they don't have the typical star-shape. Not everyone pays attention to this detail and it always interesting to collect beads based on your own criteria.

Size: L10.5 (⅜ inch) × φ8.9 (⅜ inch) (second from the right)

Bamanan tribe
Mali

UNIQUE CHEVRONS

On the left, there's a five-layer red chevron, made in Venice in the 1980s. In the middle is a six-layer green chevron. On the right, there is a brown chevron with a unique four-layer bi-cone shape.

Size: L38 (1½ inches) × φ21 (¾ inch) (left)
Size: L24 (1 inch) × φ17 (⅝ inch) (middle)
Size: L34 (1⅜ inches) × φ22 (⅞ inch) (right)

Bamanan tribe
Mali

SMALL CHEVRONS

This is a small chevron necklace. The first, third, and fourth strands from the top are antique, while the second red one and the fifth green one are from Venice in the 1980s. I also received similar items from Italian bead dealers in the early 1990s, and I used to sell them at local markets or use them for barter. I would sometimes acquire new chevron beads at the market in Bamako before traveling to the rural areas. Interestingly, blue chevrons tend to be more popular with the locals than red or green ones.

Size: L10 (⅜ inch) ×
φ8 (¼ inch)

Bamanan tribe
Mali

CHEVRON FLAT BEADS

On the left is a flat seven-layer chevron. In the upper middle is a flat six-layer green chevron. In the lower middle we have a flat seven-layer green chevron. On the right, there's a somewhat translucent five-layer chevron with four-color striped patterns.

Size: L10.5 (⅜ inch) ×
φ25.3 (1 inch) (lower middle)

Bamanan tribe
Mali

CHEVRON AND GOOSEBERRY NECKLACE

This is a mixed necklace featuring chevron and gooseberry beads obtained in Nigeria. These Venetian beads were named after the gooseberry fruit. They come in various shapes and colors (refer to p. 147).

Size: L28 (1⅛ inch) × φ23 (⅞ inch) (chevron in the foreground)

Nigeria

CHEVRON – WAVY PATTERN

These wavy-patterned beads with a white base and red and green waves are extremely rare, with very limited production. The egg-shaped one on the left was obtained in the vicinity of Bandiagara, a town of the Dogon tribe.

Size: L26 (1 inch) × φ21 (¾ inch) (left)

Bamanan tribe
Mali

CHEVRON – STRIPED PATTERN

Here are several striped chevrons on a blue base. They are rare trade beads. Unlike the beads on the left and right, the one in the middle is in good condition. This indicates that the owner took good care of it.

Size: L24 (1 inch) × φ20 (¾ inch) (left)

Dogon tribe
Mali

CHEVRON – STRIPED PATTERN

These round striped chevron beads are commonly found throughout Mali, including in Mopti, Dogon, and Bamanan tribe townships. From left we have a blue base, dark blue base, and green base striped chevron. They resemble the striped pattern of a Japanese Edo bead.

Size: L22 (⅞ inch) × φ22 (⅞ inch) (left)
Size: L20 (¾ inch) × φ21 (¾ inch) (middle)
Size: L22 (⅞ inch) × φ20 (¾ inch) (right)

Bamanan tribe
Mali

CHEVRON – STRIPED PATTERN

These are striped chevron beads, similar to the leftmost bead in the photo above. The one above was used by the Bamanan people, while these were used by the Dogon.

Size: L21 (¾ inch) × φ20 (¾ inch) (left)

Dogon tribe
Mali

CHEVRON – WAVY PATTERN

These are wavy-patterned chevron beads. There are both round and egg-shaped varieties. The large-sized multicolored bead at the back-left has three colors, while the bead in the front is of the rare two-color type. The egg-shaped beads on the right have a black base with white and red wavy patterns. For the Bamanan people, both of these beads belong to the family of "tire beads" (see p. 200).

Size: L21 (¾ inch) ×
φ22 (⅞ inch) (front left)

Bamanan tribe
Mali

UNIQUE CHEVRON

On the left is an extremely rare chevron. It has a four-color, striped pattern on a navy blue base. It features white, light blue, and brown. This bead was acquired from the Dogon people. The three on the right have three-color wavy patterns and are similar to Japanese Edo beads.

Size: L27 (1⅛ inches) ×
φ22 (⅞ inch) (left)

Left: Dogon tribe
Others: Bamanan tribe
Mali

CHEVRON – STRIPED PATTERN

On the left is a three-color chevron – white and blue with red stripes. It is known as the "American flag." The one in the middle is a simple monochrome bead, a favorite among many collectors. The one on the right, like the seven-layer chevron, has a transparent light green central hole.

Size: L16 (⅝ inch) × φ18 (¾ inch) (left)

Bamanan tribe
Mali

CHEVRON – STRIPED PATTERN

These are round chevron beads with individual stripes. They are available in various regions of Mali, including the Mopti, Dogon, and Bamanan villages.

Size: L17 (⅝ inch) × φ23 (⅞ inch) (left)

Bamanan tribe
Mali

YELLOW CHEVRON

These are rare yellow chevron beads. The beads have multiple red, black, green, and white lines drawn from the ends towards the center. They somewhat resemble striped Japanese Edo beads.

Size: L24 (1 inch) × φ16 (⅝ inch) (left)

Fulani tribe
Mali

GREEN CHEVRON

This is a light green–based chevron obtained in Mali. It has red patterns. It's a rare bead with limited production.

Size: L23 (⅞ inch) × φ17 (⅝ inch)

Dogon tribe
Mali

GREEN CHEVRON

A rare round-shaped five-layer green chevron.

Size: L25 (1 inch) × φ28 (1⅛ inches)

Bamanan tribe
Mali

REPLICA CHEVRONS

These chevrons, also known as fake chevrons, are relatively scarce and thus quite desirable to collectors. They come in four-layer, five-layer, six-layer, and seven-layer variations. Unlike standard chevron beads, these are made from porcelain instead of glass, which makes them lighter. The patterns are painted on the surface rather than embedded within the glass, so they may fade over time depending on storage conditions. They are available in both round and egg-shaped varieties.

Four-layer and six-layer

On the right, the pattern has obviously faded.

Size: L22 (⁷⁄₈ inch) × φ16 (⁵⁄₈ inch) (left)

Bamanan tribe
Mali

MODERN CHEVRONS

On the left is a uniquely patterned, creative chevron from the 1990s with five layers and 18 stars. In the middle, to the left, is an eight-layer chevron with 18 stars from the 1990s. In the middle, on the right, you can see a four-layer chevron with 18 stars. Finally, on the right there is a six-layer, 16-star black chevron.

Size: L45 (1¾ inches) × φ34 (1⅜ inches) (left)
Size: L38 (1½ inches) × φ29 (1¼ inches) (middle left)
Size: L36 (1⅜ inches) × φ25 (1 inch) (middle right)
Size: L48 (1⅞ inches) × φ43 (1⅝ inches) (right)

1980S CHEVRON PATTERN FLAT MILLEFIORI

These are flat millefiori beads made in Venice during the 1980s. They feature meticulously crafted, adorable chevron patterns. They are often used in casual jewelry, and many people incorporate just two or three of these beads into necklaces.

Size: L4 (⅛ inch) × φ13 (½ inch)

Mali

New chevron beads

WATERMELON BEADS

There are claims that these beads were used in the slave trade; however, there is no concrete evidence to support such claims. These beads come in numerous colors and patterns, with various shapes, such as simple stripes, chevron-style, onion-skin style, gooseberry, and more.

Size: L14 (½ inch) × φ8.1 (¼ inch)

Ghana, Nigeria

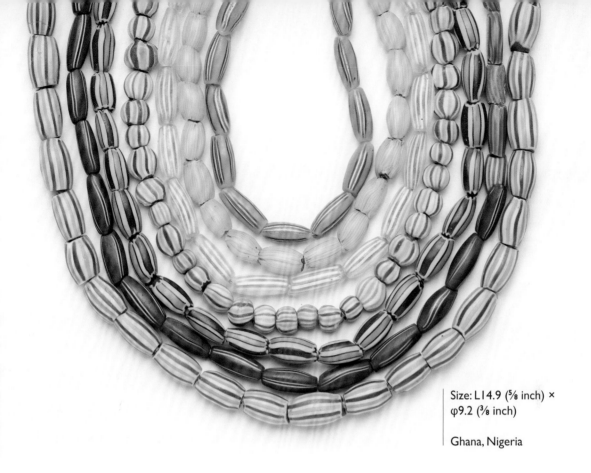

Size: L14.9 (⅝ inch) × φ9.2 (⅜ inch)

Ghana, Nigeria

GOOSEBERRY BEADS

Gooseberry beads get their charming name from their resemblance to gooseberry fruit. While this example features rare large, egg-shaped beads, they are most commonly found in small sizes. These beads come in various colors, sizes, and shapes and date back to the 18th century.

Size: L16 (⅝ inch) × φ12 (½ inch)

Nigeria

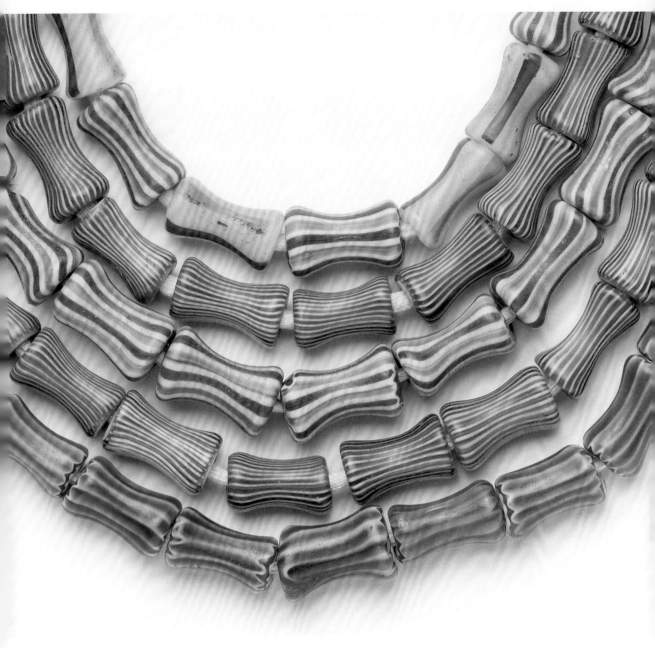

Striped

Striped

Chevron-type

MELON BEADS, DOG BONE BEADS

Among the charming melon beads, dog bone beads are the most in demand due to their scarcity. These are Ghana trade beads made in Venice. They come in a variety of patterns and colors and can be found in different types, including striped, onion-skin–type, gooseberry-type, and chevron-type beads.

Size: L13.9 (½ inch) × φ8.8 (⅜ inch)

Ghana, Nigeria

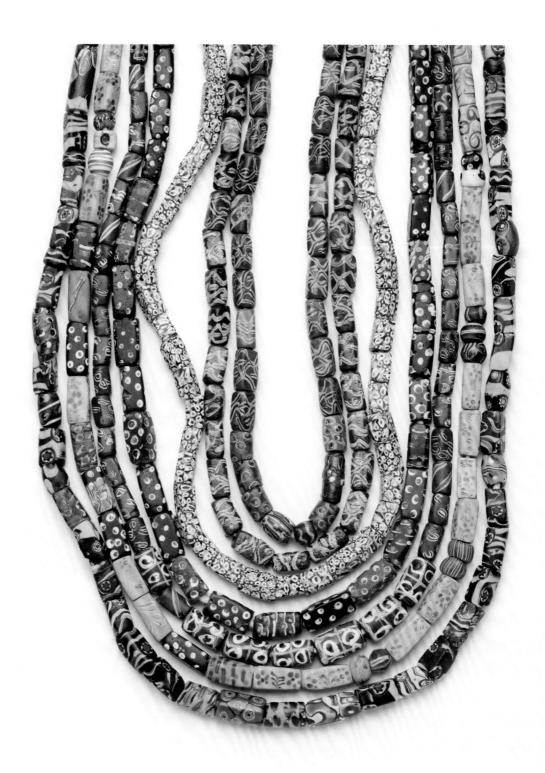

TIATIATIO – BRICK SHAPE

These beads are commonly known as millefiori – meaning "a thousand flowers" – due to their beautiful patterns. However, in Mali, they are called *Tiatiatio*. Produced in Venice during the 19th century, they made their way to Africa and are mainly found in Ghana and the Côte d'Ivoire. They come in various patterned brick shapes and are referred to as "brick trade beads" in English.

Size: L21.1 (⅞ inch) × φ10.2 (⅜ inch)

Ghana

TIATIATIO – BANANA SHAPE

These are various banana beads. They are sometimes called "elbow beads" because of their elbow-like bends. The red single-colored beads are from 19th-century Czechoslovakia production and are sometimes called "coral beads" because of their resemblance to coral.

Size: L33.3 (1¼ inches) × φ7.6 (¼ inch)

Côte d'Ivoire

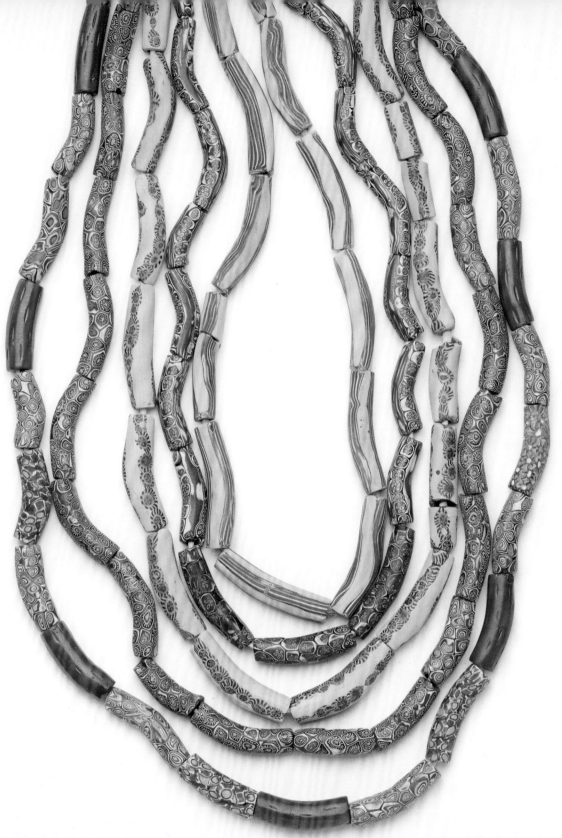

TIATIATIO – BANANA SHAPE

These banana beads are from Côte d'Ivoire.

Size: L47.5 (1⅞ inches) ×
φ11.8 (½ inch)

Côte d'Ivoire

TIATIATIO

Regular-sized millefiori.

Size: L30 (1¼ inches) ×
φ12 (½ inch)

Ghana

TIATIATIO – BANANA SHAPE

Large-sized, banana-shaped elbow beads.

Size: L55 (2⅛ inches) × φ14 (½ inch)

Côte d'Ivoire

TIATIATIO – BANANA SHAPE

One of the most common trade beads, the *Tiatiatio* is quite popular. These banana-shaped beads were obtained in Côte d'Ivoire.

Size: L59 (2⅜ inches) × φ13 (½ inch) (left front)

Côte d'Ivoire

155

VENETIAN MILLEFIORI

These elegant millefiori beads are made using delicate techniques and are designed for African trade, although some were made for the European market. The beads shown here made their way to Mali and Mauritania in West Africa.

Size: L16.4 (⅝ inch) × φ19.6 (¾ inch) (round bead on second strand, at center)

a	b
c	d
e	f

a. Halved beads, created to be gaming beads.
b. A large, flat bead.
c. Round beads.
d.–f. Various beads.

VENETIAN MILLEFIORI

The charming millefiori beads above were created using delicate and advanced techniques. They come in various sizes, but most are round or oval. Larger beads are rare and trade at high prices.

Size: L29.1 (1¼ inches) × φ19.2 (¾ inch)

Mali, Mauritania

HEXAGONAL BEADS

Hexagonal beads are found in Ghana and Côte d'Ivoire. In Côte d'Ivoire, they are also called *Kalao* beads. They are a type of millefiori bead with various patterns.

Size: L27 (1⅛ inches) × φ9 (⅜ inch)

Côte d'Ivoire

FLOWER BEADS

As the name suggests, these are flower-patterned beads. Flower beads come in a wide variety of types and captivate many people. Those with raised flower patterns are especially popular.

Size: L13.4 (½ inch) × φ16 (⅝ inch)

Fulani tribe, Bamanan tribe
Mali

FLOWER BEADS, WHITE HEARTS–TYPE DOT BEADS

The outermost strand consists of inlaid flower beads. The patterns are made with embedded glass. Those with raised flower patterns are particularly popular. They are white heart flower beads. The innermost three strands are dot beads.

Size: L11.4 (½ inch) × φ14.4 (½ inch)

Mali, Nigeria, Ethiopia, etc.

White heart flower beads with white centers.

VENETIAN BEADS – FOR EUROPEAN MARKET

These are Venetian flower beads made for the European market. They are more elaborate when compared to those that were sent to Africa. They also feature the use of gold.

Size: L24.5 (1 inch) × φ16.5 (⅝ inch) (pink bead on outermost strand)

Europe

LAMP BEADS

These are large lamp beads with a wavy pattern and are relatively rare. They were acquired in Mali.

Size: L28 (1⅛ inch) × φ19 (¾ inch) (right)

Mali

VENETIAN BEADS – LARGE SIZE

This large bead arrived in West Africa from Italy in the 1990s. Such beads were initially traded amongst dealers and later acquired by tourists and dealers from Europe and the United States.

Size: L45 (1¾ inches) × φ23 (⅞ inch)

Italy

LACE BEADS

These are lace beads that made their way to Nigeria. These fragile beads are relatively rare blown glass beads and are known for their rich variety of colors and patterns. They come in both solid-colored spiral patterns and cross spiral patterns. These are among the larger-sized trade beads.

Size: L99 (3 ⅞ inches) × φ18 (¾ inch) (front)

Nigeria

BLOWN GLASS BEADS

These are blown glass beads, similar to the lace beads on the opposite page.
They were obtained in Nigeria.

Size: L36 (1⅜ inches) ×
φ20 (¾ inch) (front)

Nigeria

WEDDING CAKE

These beads are known as "wedding cake" and are made in Venice. They also made their way to Nigeria. They are a rare tubular shape.

Size: L12 (½ inch) × φ10 (⅜ inch)

Nigeria

FANCY EYE BEADS

These yellow eye beads created through Venetian lamp work techniques were found in Ghana.

Size: L9 (⅜ inch) × φ14 (½ inch)

Ghana

TIATIATIO – COLON

In Mali, these beads belong to the *Tiatiatio* family but are not as popular or valuable as *Tiatiatio* beads.

Size: L32 (1¼ inches) × φ12 (½ inch)

Mali

NUEVA CADIZ BEADS

The oldest of these beads was excavated in Nueva Cadiz, a Spanish territory in Venezuela. In the late 18th century, Nueva Cadiz beads were once again produced for the African market. Their primary color is blue, but they also come in aqua, green, and other colors. They come in various shapes, including rectangles and twisted shapes.

Size: L36 (1⅜ inches) × φ15 (⅝ inch) (front left)
Size: L77 (3 inches) × φ14 (½ inch) (back)
Size: L71 (2¾ inches) × φ14 (½ inch) (middle right)

Nigeria

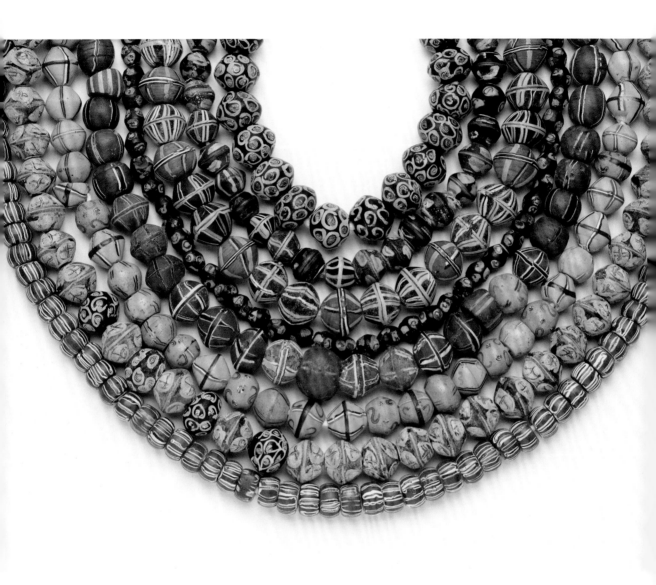

KING BEADS – ABACUS BEADS

King beads, as the name suggests, were favored by royalty and the wealthy.
These trade beads are believed to be of Venetian or Dutch origin and are
characterized by their distinctive bi-cone shape.

Size: L18 (¾ inch) ×
φ21 (⅞ inch)

Côte d'Ivoire, Mali,
Ghana, etc.

KING BEADS – MIXED

King beads come in various patterns and sizes. They can be found throughout West Africa, but Ghana is where they are most common, followed by Côte d'Ivoire. Due to their shape, some people in Japan refer to them as "abacus beads."

Size: L10 (⅜ inch) × φ20 (¾ inch)

Ghana

SKUNK RAISED DOT BEADS

These beads are named after the skunk because of their resemblance to the smelly mammal. They come in a wide range of colors, from blue, to yellow, to pink, to green, and more. White is the primary base color, but there are also beads with yellow, red, or black as their base. There are also beads with matching base and dot colors, such as red or yellow, with raised dots. This characteristic distinguishes them from the dot beads on p. 174.

Size: L12.7 (½ inch) × φ13.4 (½ inch)

Nigeria

YELLOW SKUNK RAISED DOT BEADS

These are yellow single-colored beads of the skunk raised dot variety. They come in both extra-large and small sizes.

Size: L20 (¾ inch) × φ20 (¾ inch)

Mali

DOT BEADS

Dot beads are predominantly white and black but also include variations like thousand dot beads, which have numerous tiny dots densely arranged on the outer side of black beads. These beads were originally crafted in Venice and have been used in various parts of Africa, the Americas, and Asia.

Size: L6.4 (¼ inch) × φ11.2 (½ inch)

Nigeria, Ghana, Mali, Ethiopia

FEATHER BEADS

Feather beads derive their name from their resemblance to bird feathers.
Prototypes for these beads, like the ones from the Islamic Golden Age shown
on p. 95, date back to that era. These feather beads are Venetian-made and
come from the 19th century.

Size: L14.8 (⅝ inch) ×
φ8.6 (⅜ inch) (right)

Ghana

FEATHER BEADS

These antique feather beads were made in Venice in the 19th century. They come in various shapes, including long and round beads. Although rarer, there are also flat and rectangular varieties. They are available in numerous colors, such as green, red, white, black, yellow, and more. When compared to the modern beads on p. 175 and on p. 177, these antique feather beads are more colorful and vibrant. They can be found throughout Africa.

Size: L17 (⅝ inch) × φ8 (¼ inch)

Côte d'Ivoire, Mali, Ghana, etc.

NEW FEATHER BEADS

New feather beads were created somewhere around 1990. They are considered to be the third generation of feather beads following those of the Islamic Golden Age (first generation) and the 19th-century Venetian-made beads (second generation).

Size: L26 (1 inch) × φ11.7 (½ inch) (red bead on the outer strand)

GHOST BEAD

Ghost beads get their name because their patterns resemble ghosts. Interestingly, by turning the "ghost" pattern upside down, certain patterns look like a face, so they are also known as "face beads." They are unique 19th-century Venetian-made beads.

Size: L16 (⅝ inch) × φ9 (⅜ inch)

Mali

FACE BEADS

These charming monochrome face beads are often acquired alongside *Miniyan-nuku* beads (see p. 198) in Mali. They are rarer than *Miniyan-nuku* or French ambassador beads (see p. 199), so collectors who appreciate face beads often collect only this type of bead.

Size: L24 (1 inch) × φ8 (¼ inch) (at fore)

Bamanan tribe
Mali

FACE BEADS

The old Baule face beads were produced in Italy and made their way to Africa as trade beads. They are favored by the Baule people of Côte d'Ivoire and are highly sought-after. Consequently, newly produced versions have appeared. The newer beads from the 1990s often feature round shapes, while the older versions tend to be flat.

Size: L15.1 (⅝ inch) ×
φ17.1 (⅝ inch) (right)

Baule tribe
Côte d'Ivoire

Newer Baule face beads made in India, circa 1990s.

Dutch Trade Beads

Archaeological excavations in Amsterdam's old city, particularly the filled-in canals around Waterloo Square in the former Jewish district, uncovered various glass beads, glass chunks, and glass rods dating from the late 16th century. Excavations near the Keizersgracht Canal revealed over 50,000 drawn glass beads and bead fragments from the same period.

In the mid-16th century, Venetian glassworkers came to the Netherlands to work. Besides Amsterdam, bead production took place in a variety of other Dutch cities, including Haarlem, Zutphen, Utrecht, Rotterdam, The Hague, Delft, and Middelburg. The beads were transported by Dutch, English, and French explorers and merchants to North America, South Africa, West Africa, and Indonesia.

In 1609, Englishman Henry Hudson arrived in North America as a representative of the Dutch East India Company. During his journey, he exchanged "beads, knives, and hatchets" as barter items with indigenous peoples. As a result, the exchanged beads were known as Dutch beads.

While some Dutch beads resemble Venetian beads in their opulence, others, like the white hearts, have a simpler appearance. Dutch beads have found their way into various cultures worldwide and have been cherished by many people over the centuries.

DUDU

Dudu beads are representative of the Dogon people. They come in various sizes, and each one is characterized by its single gentle and soothing shade. Standard *Dudu* beads are round and are primarily blue or white, though you can also find them in yellow, navy blue, light blue, and various transparent variations. Besides round beads, there are also tube-shaped *Dudu* beads and dome-shaped gaming beads.

Some dome-shaped gaming beads were actually reformed large beads and are quite rare. These beads, often known as "Dogon blue" or "Dogon cobalt blue," come in various sizes and can be round, oval, or tubular. Those who appreciate glass beads may notice a striking resemblance between *Dudu* beads and traditional Ainu beads from Japan. Ainu beads are said to have been produced during the Edo period (1603–1868) in both Edo and China. It's rather intriguing that the two distant cultures of the Ainu and the Dogon had such similar tastes for these items.

Size: L39.3 (1½ inches) × φ22.7 (⅞ inch)

Dogon tribe
Mali

Size: L28 (1⅛ inches) ×
φ20.9 (¾ inch)

Dogon tribe
Mali

THE UNIQUE WORLDVIEW OF THE DOGON PEOPLE

The Dogon people reside in the Mopti region of central Mali. While the Dogon are most famous for their dwellings around the Bandiagara Escarpment, their society is actually composed of over 700 villages in and around the entire Bandiagara region. Historically, the Dogon people inhabited the region known as Manden in the Mali Empire. However, the Dogon people are known for avoiding conflict and escaping from Islamic domination to preserve their unique culture and traditions. They chose to settle in the Bandiagara Escarpment, an area that is far from hospitable.

The Bandiagara Escarpment was previously inhabited by the Tellem people (hereafter Tellem). There is a misconception that the Dogon people expelled the Tellem from the area when they moved in, but this is not the case. The Dogon people actually consider the Tellem to be their ancestors, meaning that they accepted and had gratitude toward their predecessors. It was the Dogon people who popularized the term "Tellem," which means "those who were here before us" in the Dogon language.

The Tellem were primarily hunters and gatherers, while the Dogon were farmers. There were differences in their ways of life, but they coexisted for some time. Over the years, some Tellem moved away, while others remained and integrated with the Dogon, resulting in a blend of both cultures that shaped the current Dogon culture.

Distinctive architectural features in Dogon villages include the unique carved columns, called *Toguna*, and sturdy roofed meeting halls. These meeting halls are where crucial discussions concerning the village are held. Inside the *Toguna*, people are expected to remain calm. To prevent haste and disruptions, the entrance is narrow. The ceiling is also low to discourage people from standing up or engaging in unruly behavior. This design, with limited access and the requirement to sit, served the function of preventing conflict.

Mali is known for having some of the strongest indigenous and nature-based beliefs in Africa. Traditional beliefs were upheld among the different ethnic groups in Mali, such as the Dogon and the Bamanan. Actually, these same beliefs were preserved even among those who may identify as Muslim or Christian, suggesting a profound continuity of indigenous belief systems.

The Dogon people have a unique and extremely interesting worldview and mythology. According to their beliefs, their ancestors descended from the heavens bearing grain, which, when cultivated, had the power to purify the earth's impurities.

As an agricultural society, the Dogon place great importance on their grain storehouses, where they keep their food supplies. Similar to high-floored storehouses in the Yayoi period (10th century to 3rd century BCE) of Japan, these granaries are elevated above the ground. Access to the granaries requires a famous ladder-like object that is essential to Dogon life.

The Dogon have several important festivals, including *Dama* and the more significant *Sigui*. *Sigui* is a grand event that occurs only once every 60 years. Over a seven-year period, the *Sigui* festival involves much more than just celebrations. It serves as a period to pass on Dogon culture and traditions to the younger generation who will lead for the next 60 years. The Dogon, being an agricultural society, avoid holding the festival during the rainy season. The last *Sigui* festival was held from 1967 to 1974, but the upcoming *Sigui* festival in 2027 is an eagerly awaited event for researchers and enthusiasts of Dogon culture worldwide.

Masks and dances are essential to Dogon society. They have over 80 different types of masks, with the *Kanaga* mask usually making its appearance first in their dances. Other masks include the *Satimbe*, *Walu*, *Sirigé*, and more.

The Dogon people possess a unique worldview and a strong sense of aesthetics. Beads are indispensable for expressing these elements.

Photos: Dogon people and a festival scene

Size: L5.9 (¼ inch) ×
φ11.3 (½ inch)

Dogon tribe
Mali

Left: Regular beads
Right: Excavated beads

Size: L20 (¾ inch) × φ23 (⅞ inch) (navy
blue bead right of center on left strand)

Dogon tribe
Mali

Size: L27 (1⅛ inches) × φ14 (½ inch)

Dogon tribe
Mali

Size: L7 (¼ inch) × φ10 (⅜ inch)

Dogon tribe
Mali

Size: L17.8 (¾ inch)
× φ24.3 (1 inch)

Dogon tribe
Mali

Size: L20.7 (¾ inch) ×
φ24.1 (1 inch)

Dogon tribe
Mali

Locally, these beads are also referred to as *Kadjolo* beads.

Size: L9 (⅜ inch) ×
φ16 (⅝ inch)

Dogon tribe
Mali

DOGON DONUTS

Dogon donuts come primarily in cobalt blue (Dogon blue) and clear. Due to their popularity among enthusiasts these beads have a variety of names, such as Dogon donuts, Dogon disks, Dogon ring beads, and Dogon tire beads. The photo depicts a rare, thin, purple-colored Dogon donut. The green and orange beads on the right page also employ rare colors. Old Dogon donuts in green and orange are no longer readily available on the market. Most of the green and orange Dogon donuts available today are quite lovely new beads.

Size: L4 (⅛ inch) × φ13 (½ inch)

Dogon tribe
Mali

Size: L4.7 (⅛ inch) ×
φ12.9 (½ inch)

Dogon tribe
Mali

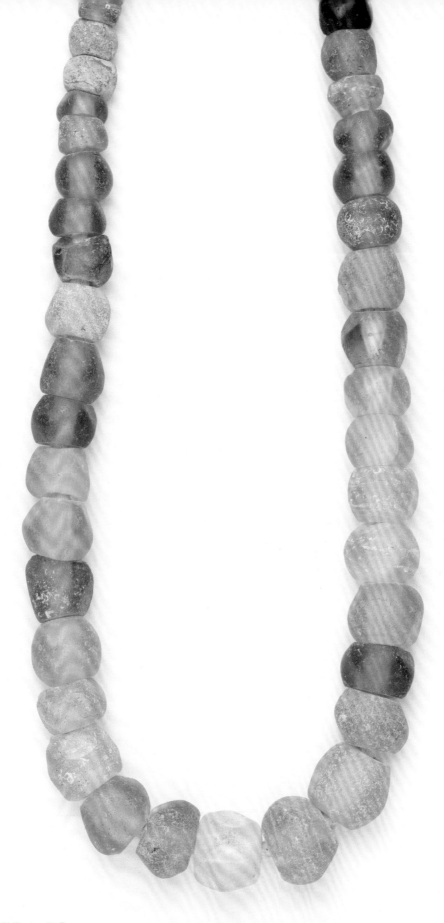

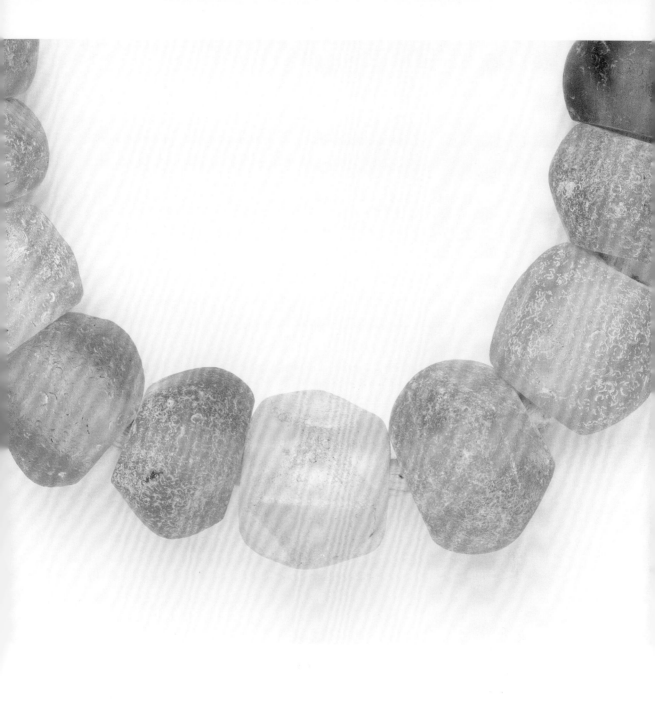

DOGON TELEVISION

This bead is famous in Mali and is known as the "Dogon television." It dates back to the 18th century and is a German-made, hand-cut, bead. The larger the bead, the more valuable it is. White, clear, and purple colors are popular, while orange and blue variations are extremely rare.

Size: L20.6 (¾ inch) × φ22.5 (⅞ inch)

Dogon tribe
Mali

WHITE HEARTS

White hearts are some of the most commonly found glass beads worldwide. The white portion around the bead hole is often likened to a heart. While red is the standard color, you can also find them in navy blue, green, yellow, light blue, brown, and more.

Similar to chevron beads, white hearts are still being produced today. These trade beads are frequently used in jewelry making. They come in various sizes, including large, medium, and small, with a variety of shapes, including round and tubular.

In addition to standard white hearts, there are also yellow hearts and green hearts. Note that green hearts and green white hearts are distinct varieties. Green hearts have a green center.

Size: L4.3 (⅛ inch) × φ5.7 (¼ inch)

Nigeria

White hearts with a white center

Green hearts with a green center

Size: L17.4 (¾ inch) ×
φ21.9 (⅞ inch)

Nigeria

SIX BEADS

These beads are called "six beads" because of the patterns that resemble the number 6. They are also known as "Zen beads" because their patterns resemble a circular symbol drawn by Zen monks. These beads tend to be of Dutch origin, but they are said to have been produced in Germany as well. They come in various colors, including black, and more rarely, white, red, blue, green, and yellow, among others.

Size: L10 (⅜ inch) × φ11 (½ inch)

Mali

Multicolor six beads

Size: L15.6 (⅝ inch) ×
φ16.1 (⅝ inch) (black
bead at center)

Nigeria, Mali,
Burkina Faso, etc.

MINIYAN-NUKU (SNAKE INTESTINES)

In the Bamanan language, *Miniyan-nuku* means "snake's intestines." In the Western context, these beads are referred to as "Lewis and Clark beads." However, in Mali, nobody recognizes this name. For the Bamanan people, the *Miniyan-nuku,* French ambassador beads, and tire beads all belong to the same family.

Size: L27 (1⅛ inches) × φ10 (⅜ inch)

Bamanan tribe
Mali

FRENCH AMBASSADOR BEADS

In Africa, there is a legend that French ambassadors' wives liked these beads and used to buy them often. In the United States, it's also said that American ambassadors either presented these beads to the local people or received them as gifts, but there doesn't seem to be any credible evidence to support these claims.

Size: L23 (⅞ inch) ×
φ18 (¾ inch)

Bamanan tribe
Mali

New French ambassador beads made in India around 1990.

TIRE BEADS

The upper part of the necklace features French ambassador beads, while the lower part contains coral beads placed between tire beads. The tire beads family includes *Miniyan-nuku* and French ambassador beads. Tire beads themselves are relatively scarce. They are named for their resemblance to the shape of a car tire.

Size: L9.2 (⅜ inch) × φ24.7 (1 inch)

Bamanan tribe
Mali

FEATHER BEAD

To the left we see a large, clear, egg-shaped orange bead with beautiful feather-like gold foil patterns. Near the hole, you can see four wavy colored patterns embedded in the bead. This wavy white, blue, and red pattern is often referred to as the "American flag" pattern.

Size: L33 (1¼ inches) × φ21 (¾ inch)

Mali

FEATHER BEADS

These scarce feather beads have feather-like patterns around the center of each bead. Feather beads have been produced for a long time, dating all the way back to ancient times.

Size: L35 (1⅜ inches) × φ14 (½ inch) (left)
Size: L31 (1¼ inches) × φ14 (½ inch) (right)

Bamanan tribe
Mali

FANCY FEATHER BEAD

This is a flat, mosaic feather bead. This particular example is a fancy feather bead from the 19th century. Flat fancy beads like this are relatively rare and are favored by many.

Size: L14.1 (½ inch) × φ16.5 (⅝ inch)

Bamanan tribe
Mali

UNIQUE BEADS

The one on the left is a unique chevron-type bead. Both ends are cut and polished. Some beads are extremely rare, with only a few found throughout the world, and sometimes only a single example exists. These two beads are such rare finds.

Size: L41 (1⅝ inches) × φ14 (½ inch) (left)
Size: L26 (1 inch) × φ19 (¾ inch) (right)

Fulani tribe
Mali

FANCY BEADS

These are rare Dutch-made glass beads.

Size: L47 (1⅞ inches) × φ9 (⅜ inch) (left)
Size: L23 (⅞ inch) × φ14 (½ inch) (second from left)

Bamanan tribe
Mali

FANCY BEADS

Above we see beads of various colors and shapes.

Size: L11 (½ inch) × φ8 (¼ inch) (center front)

Mali

Czech Beads

Czech glass beads are known to have been produced in Bohemia and Moravia from the 10th century. This region was relatively isolated from the densely populated areas of Europe, which put them at a commercial disadvantage. However, the vast northern forests provided inexpensive fuel and ash needed for glass production, helping to offset the cost of transporting beads over long distances.

By the 17th century, the people of Bohemia decided to start making their own beads. Bohemians and Moravians learned Venetian beadmaking techniques and developed more efficient methods for mass-producing molded beads. By the end of the 17th century, their bead industry was substantial enough to trade with foreign nations. From the mid-18th century, their beads were traded globally, including in Africa.

Bohemians and Moravians also specialized in replicating beads and bead materials, used in other parts of the world, with glass. In the 19th century they replicated Indian beads made from agate and carnelian, as well as African beads made from shells, bones, and coral, and exported these replicas to Africa. These glass replicas, in addition to their dazzling glass beauty, were more affordable to produce when compared to beads made from the original natural materials, making them economically attractive to people in Africa.

Czech beads are known for their single-color beads and the diverse shapes created through molding. This gives them a distinct and intriguing character different from Venetian and Dutch beads.

WEDDING BEADS (*SOKINAN*)

Wedding beads are cherished by the Soninke women living in Mali. They come in vivid and chromatic colors and are often worn on joyous occasions such as weddings and birthdays, which is how they got the name "wedding beads." They are also affectionately called lightbulb beads because they resemble lightbulbs. In English, they are known as teardrop beads. These beads are molded using Bohemian glass and come in about six different shapes and countless patterns.

The photo shows a standard necklace made of wedding beads. Most people usually prefer to have various shapes and colors mixed in a single necklace, as depicted here.

Size: L23.7 (⅞ inch) × φ13.8 (½ inch) (yellow striped bead, lower center)

Soninke tribe
Mali

Collectible necklaces featuring teardrop-shaped and flat beads of the same, or similar, colors.

Size: L6 (¼ inch) × φ12 (½ inch)

Soninke tribe
Mali

TRIANGLE-SHAPED AND COMMA-SHAPED (HOOKED) BEADS

Size: L30 (1¼ inches) ×
H35 (1⅜ inches) × D3
(⅛ inch)

Soninke tribe
Mali

Locally, necklaces usually don't consist of just one type or color. This is a collectible necklace (a strand intended for a bead collection that consists of similar beads) that has been assembled by actually disassembling multiple necklaces. Only the triangle and comma-shaped beads are then strung back together.

Size: L12 (½ inch) ×
H18 (¾ inch) (blue)

Soninke tribe
Mali

Wedding beads – Flat: Small, lovely, flat wedding beads.

Size: L13.2 (½ inch) ×
φ9.2 (⅜ inch) (center
yellow-green)

Soninke tribe
Mali

Wedding beads – Teardrop-shape: Cute, small teardrop wedding beads. This is a collectible bead set separated by pattern.

Size: L8.8 (³⁄₈ inch) × φ11.9 (½ inch)
(dark red bead at center-bottom)

Soninke tribe
Mali

Wedding Beads – Standard: These are typical multi-colored small teardrop-shaped wedding beads.

Size: L28.6 (1⅛ inches)
× φ17.9 (¾ inch) (white
bead at left-center)

Soninke tribe
Mali

Wedding Beads – Large: These are relatively large wedding beads and, unlike other wedding beads, each has a single color.

URANIUM BEADS

These are 19th-century Bohemian uranium beads from Czechoslovakia. In the United States, they are known as vaseline beads. In Japan, they are sometimes called abacus beads. Others sometimes refer to them as diamond beads. These beads were produced for a relatively short period and in limited quantities, so some colors like white, clear, and orange are rare. Yellow is the most common color. These beads exhibit a beautiful, iridescent glow when exposed to ultraviolet light.

Size: L5.9 (¼ inch) × φ9.6 (⅜ inch)

Mali

Size: L14.1 (½ inch) ×
φ15.7 (⅝ inch)

Mali

Size: L11.7 (½ inch) ×
φ15.5 (⅝ inch)

Mali

CUT BEADS

These are Bohemian glass beads from the Czech Republic. One distinctive feature of Bohemian glass is its simplicity and solid colors, which gives these beads a charming quality. These particular beads are octagonally cut and come primarily in large and small sizes, with some medium-sized beads thrown in. Available colors include ruby red, transparent white, opal, green, blue, orange, and white.

Size: L22 (⅞ inch) × φ14 (½ inch) (green in the center)

Mali, Burkina Faso, Nigeria, etc.

213

SA-KOLO

Snake beads are a masterpiece of Czech-made Bohemian glass. When strung on a cord, they resemble real bones. They are known by various names due to their immense popularity. In Mali, they are called *Sa-Kolo*. In addition to the term "snake beads," they are also known as *sekizuitama* (snake bones) in Japan, and vertebrae beads, spine beads or snake spine beads in Europe and the United States. They come in various sizes and colors, including white, black, pink, navy-blue, yellow, red, blue, and more. The original design was inspired by the vertebrae of actual snakes. Some older versions are made of metal (refer to p. 38).

Size: L4.5 (⅛ inch) × φ8.9 (⅜ inch)

Mali, Burkina Faso, Nigeria, etc.

Size: L4.9 (⅛ inch) ×
φ8.5 (⅜ inch)

Mali, Burkina Faso,
Nigeria, etc.

DICE BEADS

Dice beads, also known as cube beads, are Czech-made dot beads. They are primarily found in the shape of a cube and come in various colors, such as black, blue, and red. Dice beads made their way not only to Africa but also to Asian regions like Tibet. They have been cherished as necklace beads, player beads and prayer beads in some regions.

Size: L8.2 (¼ inch) × φ7.3 (¼ inch)

Nigeria

BOHEMIAN FLOWER BEADS

These charming beads are known as Bohemian Flowers and exude an intrinsic sense of fun and fascination. Although not evident, when strung together these beads are shaped like four-leaf clovers. They come in various sizes, numerous colors, and diverse shapes. The brown beads third from the top also show an intriguing method of connection.

Bohemian artisans were dedicated not only to creating beads for business, but also to creating beads that were enjoyable, interesting, practical, and culturally and religiously significant.

Size: L4.1 (⅛ inch) × φ8.1 (¼ inch) (black)

Ghana, Mali, Nigeria, etc.

ETHIOPIAN CHERRY BEADS

These beads are found all over Ethiopia and received their name from their resemblance to delicious cherries. They come in various sizes and are mostly found in various shades of red, but you can also find yellow, orange, and other colors. In West Africa, particularly in Mali and Burkina Faso, there are similar, smaller beads. In Mali, there's a bead known as *Kono Fan*, which means "dove's egg." In English, Ethiopian cherry beads are referred to as pigeon egg beads.

Size: L22 (⅞ inch) × φ18 (¾ inch)

Ethiopia

ETHIOPIAN CHERRY

Ethiopian cherry beads come in various colors and sizes, ranging from dark red to yellow. Many of these beads have an opaque appearance.

Size: L27.7 (1⅛ inches) × φ23 (⅞ inch)

Ethiopia

KONO FAN

These are *Kono Fan* beads obtained from the Bamanan people in Mali. Similar to Ethiopian cherry beads, these are Czech-made. The Malian *Kono Fan* beads on the left have a matte finish and resemble the Bohemian coral beads on p. 223. The beads from Burkina Faso on the right are more transparent.

Size: L18 (¾ inch) × φ13 (½ inch) (left)
Size: L9 (⅜ inch) × φ9 (⅜ inch) (right)

Bamanan tribe
Left: Mali, Right: Burkina Faso

MECCA BEADS

Mecca beads are Bohemian-made and hold great cultural significance for Islamic believers. Muslims acquire these beads as proof of their pilgrimage to Mecca. They are all flat and, unlike typical glass beads, they become a part of the wearer, providing a sense of gentleness to the body. Larger Mecca beads may have Arabic script on them, while smaller ones may feature depictions of the moon and stars or include single written characters. The predominant color is ruby red, but they can also be found in white, black, blue, and orange.

Size: L33 (1¼ inches) × W25 (1 inch)

Nigeria

BOHEMIAN CORAL

Here's a variety of Bohemian coral beads. Czech-made coral beads come in various sizes and shapes, including large, medium, and small round beads, tube-shaped beads, banana-shaped beads, and faceted beads.

Size: L29 (1¼ inches) × φ14 (½ inch)

Mali

BOHEMIAN CORAL

This is a strand of beads made in Bohemia, known as Bohemian coral due to their resemblance to coral. These vintage faux coral beads have a simple and gentle coloration. The strand includes various shapes, from round, to drop shaped, to dog-bone shaped.

Size: L7 (¼ inch) × φ12 (½ inch)

Mali

223

BOHEMIAN DOG BONE

These Bohemian dog bone beads share design similarities with snake beads and Bohemian flower beads. The addition of patterns makes them even more intriguing. These beads come with both horizontal and vertical holes.

Size: L7.3 (¼ inch) × φ16.6 (⅝ inch)

Nigeria, Ghana

BAYA BEADS

Baya Beads are essential waist beads for women in various West African countries, including Mali and Senegal. They are unique to Africa and are used to attract men, and they are still highly valued in various parts of Africa. In Mali, they are called Baya. In Senegal, they go by *Binbin* or *Djaldjal*. In Nigeria, they are known as *Ileke*, *Jigida*. Finally, in Kenya they are referred to as *Shanga*. Baya beads often play a romantic role, acting as aphrodisiac-like glass beads during intimate moments between couples.

Size: L6 (¼ inch) × φ7 (¼ inch)

Bamanan tribe
Mali

225

BEADS MADE IN GERMANY AND OTHER COUNTRIES

GERMAN MARBLE

German marble beads are rare. They don't differ much from regular large marbles except for the presence of a hole. They were initially produced as regular marbles in the 19th century before making their way to Africa and Asia as trade beads. Due to their limited production and rarity, they have become a luxury item. Nigeria is one of the primary destinations of these beads. They come in various sizes and patterns, including solid colors and two-tone variations.

Size: L17 (⅝ inch) × φ18 (¾ inch) (left)

Nigeria

The German marble and green chevron beads are from Nigeria. The rest were obtained in Mali.

Size: L35.7 (1⅜ inches) × φ37.3 (1½ inches)

Nigeria, Mali

Size: L23 (⅞ inch) × φ25.1
(1 inch) (left-center, round
bead on outer strand)

Nigeria

Mixed German marbles

Even with its cracks, this is a beautiful marble bead.

Nigeria

STRIPED COPAL

A beautiful, color-separated, double-stranded collectible copal. The brown strand consists of large beads that have irregular stripes. These stripes aren't actually cracks. This makes them a rare find.

COPAL

These are imitations of amber made in Germany during the colonial period. Originally, copal referred to amber that has not fully fossilized. However, we also use the term copal to refer to beads made of synthetic resin during the colonial period. Collectors in Europe, the United States, Japan, and Taiwan often prefer this synthetic amber. While natural amber has been used by ancient people in its simple, natural form, copal has been shaped by modern people, enhancing its beauty. Furthermore, over time, copal develops colors that mature and, depending on your perspective, can have a charm similar to natural amber.

Size: L27.1 (1⅛ inches) × φ38.8 (1½ inches)

Fulani tribe
Mali

EXTRA-LARGE COPAL

These are unusual and beautiful extra-large copal beads. This is a single strand collected painstakingly in Mali, featuring large beads that are truly unique.

Size: L43.6 (1¾ inches) × φ54.4 (2⅛ inches)

Fulani tribe
Mali

DOGON RED AMBER

These beautiful beads known as Dogon amber were obtained in Mali. They are quite scarce among copal beads and command a high price. Even though they are resin-based, Dogon amber is generally referred to simply as "amber."

Size: L10 (⅜ inch) × φ25 (1 inch)

Dogon tribe
Mali

COPAL NECKLACE

These copal beads, five in total, are from Nepal. They are of the same type as the copal beads that originated from Africa.

Left: Contemporary necklace with plastic amber and Djenné beads

Right: Contemporary necklace with plastic amber and Tuareg beads

Both items were obtained in Mali.

AMBER AND SYNTHETIC AMBER

AMBER (NATURAL)
Amber is fossilized natural resin, typically from trees like pine and spruce.

COPAL (NATURAL)
Copal is a semi-fossilized resin that is younger than amber. Its molecular bonds are weaker compared to amber and it contains volatile components, which cause it to melt at lower temperatures and produces a different fragrance than amber. Like amber, copal sometimes has small insects encased in it. The word "copal" originates from the Nahuatl word *copalli*, meaning "incense." Many indigenous groups in Mexico still use copal as incense.

AMBROID (RECONSTITUTED NATURAL)
Reconstituted amber, called "ambroid," is produced by subjecting amber pieces to heat and pressure in a mold to compact them.

BAKELITE, RESOL RESIN, NOVOLAK (SYNTHETIC)
These synthetic resins were used extensively in German factories to mass-produce imitation amber. However, these resins are no longer used in the production of imitation amber.

PHENOLIC RESIN (SYNTHETIC)
Phenolic resin was most commonly used in the production of synthetic amber. Its primary color is deep red, but lighter brown and yellow beads were also manufactured. The highly regarded "cherry amber" in Ethiopia is made from deep red phenolic resin.

CELLULOID (SYNTHETIC)
Celluloid is an imitation amber made from nitrocellulose. It is yellow and often cloudy and is highly flammable.

CASEIN (SYNTHETIC)
Casein is a synthetic resin made from milk. Imitation amber made from casein is a cloudy, opaque yellow. It was also used as an alternative to ivory. Amber imitations have been created from various materials, including animal horns, bones, and glass. Many synthetic plastic imitations derived from petroleum are prevalent today.

Regarding the items introduced on pp. 230–234, which we refer to as "copal" or "imitation amber," it's unclear which specific resin each one is made from.

I acquired the large imitation amber pieces about a decade before coming to Japan. That means they were available approximately 30 years ago.

A woman wearing a large imitation amber necklace. This resembles the Moroccan-made piece mentioned above.

Contemporary plastic amber

1. On the left is a young woman dressed in Fulani style. On the right is a young woman in the Bamanan style.

2. A baby wearing a bead bracelet. Around her neck we see a necklace of white glass beads. Both serve as protective talismans.

3. A woman wearing glass beads.

4. On the left is my father, Traore Mamadou, and next to him are my uncles. Wearing amber is my youngest sister.

5. On the left, Mr. Baba Cisse, the owner of the bead museum in Mopti, wearing cowrie shells and a large round Baule brass necklace.

1. A popular jewelry shop.

2. This coachman is wearing an interesting cowrie shell necklace, but the focus is on the headdress of the woman sitting inside the carriage behind him.

3. This coachman was spotted in Mopti. His bag is decorated with cowrie shells and his shoes are embellished with cowrie shells.

4. The riverside in Mopti.

1. Amadou is a young man who searches for beads in a rural area. According to him, the number of beads available in a single day at market is so limited that it wouldn't even fill one pocket. Sometimes, he has to travel tens of kilometers from the main roads to remote regions where neither buses nor tourists go. He uses a horse-drawn cart called a "charette" and says that acquiring beads is not an easy task.

2.–6. Some beads Amadou acquired.

7. & 8. Beads are most often gathered one by one, then grouped into strands of the same type.

9. These are *Tiatiatio* beads. They are plentiful in Ghana, so strands with various sizes and colors can be easily created.

10. In Mali, *Tiatiatio* beads are scarce, so they are combined with various other beads to form a strand.

1. & 2. Agate and amber rings

3. & 4. Large amulet necklaces adorned with beads.

5. An original necklace of amber.

6. Raffia and cowrie-shell beadwork on a Congo basket.

7. A stool adorned with Kuba cloth and beadwork using cowrie shells.

African Beads in Modern Times

During the colonial era, many trade beads came into Africa from Europe, but the continent also had its own glass bead-making traditions. Glass bead production, especially after the 16th century, was concentrated in West Africa, particularly in Nigeria and Ghana, south of the Sahara.

Some beads that were once made in West Africa are no longer produced today. Notable among these are the Bodom beads and Akosu beads, which were highly valued in West Africa and were manufactured in Ghana from the 19th to the 20th century. Also produced during the same period were Kiffa beads, seen on the right. Production of these beads had ceased for a time but have experienced a revival in recent times. Bead-making traditions have been passed down until today and the Yoruba people of Nigeria – along with various Ghanaian ethnic groups like the Ashanti and Krobo – continue to actively produce beads.

In African societies, mysterious and mystical powers were associated with status and authority, and blacksmiths who transformed iron ore into new forms by heating were held in high regard and awe. Kings, priests, and diviners wore iron necklaces as symbols of power. The forging of iron was associated with the ability to harness magical forces and control the powers of nature.

Other metal crafts in Africa include the goldwork of Ghana's Ashanti people, the silversmithing of Ethiopia's Oromo people, and Ethiopian Orthodox crosses. Berber and Tuareg communities also produce silver pendants. The Dogon, Yoruba, Akan, Baule, and various other ethnic groups each have their own methods of metalwork and bead production, contributing to the diversity of African beadwork.

KIFFA BEADS

These beads can be sourced from Mauritania and Mali, but they were originally crafted in Kiffa, Mauritania. Production was limited to a short period from the late 19th century to the early 20th century, making them extremely scarce. It is believed that these beads were primarily made by women. Kiffa beads come in five main shapes: Triangular teardrop, tubular, round, conical, and diamond shaped. They feature intricate patterns and a combination of colors, such as red, blue, yellow, brown, and white. Many people were involved in their production, resulting in a variety of shapes, patterns, and colors. Around the year 2000, new Kiffa beads began to be crafted in Kiffa using the old traditional techniques.

EARLY VINTAGE KIFFA BEAD

This is a vintage, standard round bead.

Size: L14 (½ inch) × φ14 (½ inch)

Origin: Mauritania

EARLY VINTAGE KIFFA BEADS

These are vintage, standard triangular Kiffa beads. They are among the most popular in the Kiffa bead category. The ones with silver additions have been repaired by the Tuareg people.

Size: L13.2 (½ inch) × H26.2 (1 inch) (left)

Mauritania

KIFFA BEAD: CONICAL SHAPE

This is a vintage, standard conical Kiffa bead, often referred to as a "gaming bead."

Size: L10.3 (⅜ inch) × φ13.2 (½ inch)

Mauritania

KIFFA BEAD: TUBULAR

Chipped antique tubular Kiffa Bead.

Size: L26.7 (1 inch) × φ10.7 (⅜ inch)

Mauritania

DROP KIFFA BEADS

These Kiffa beads include a drop-shaped blue bead with an "M" pattern and a transparent green Kiffa bead.

Size: L15.9 (⅝ inch) × W16.1 (⅝ inch) × D9.6 (⅜ inch) (left)
Size: L8.5 (⅜ inch) × W8.5 (⅜ inch) × D6.1 (¼ inch) (right)

Mauritania

OLD KIFFA BEAD

This is a transparent green Kiffa bead.

Size: L7.9 (¼ inch) × φ11.7 (½ inch)

Mauritania

KIFFA BEAD: WAVE PATTERNS

This is a transparent Kiffa bead that features round, wave-like patterns.

Size: L12.3 (½ inch) × φ15.6 (⅝ inch)

Mauritania

KIFFA BEAD STRANDS

The outer strand consists of old Kiffa beads, including silver re-made beads of the Tuareg people. The large round beads on the inner strand are new Kiffa beads.

Size: L13.2 (½ inch) × φ19 (¾ inch) (central bead on inner strand)

Mauritania

KIFFA BEADS

These are new Kiffa beads from the early 2000s.

Size: L19 (¾ inch) ×
H13 (½ inch)

Mauritania

RECYCLED BEADS, AKOSO BEADS, BODOM BEADS

On the left, we have a recycled bead. It was created by crushing old or broken beads into a powder and then reforming them into something new. These are known as "powdered glass beads." In the middle are *Akoso* beads, and on the right are *Bodom* beads. *Akoso* and *Bodom* beads were used by the noble classes, with *Akoso* being associated with the Ewe people and *Bodom* with the Ashanti people. These beads were believed to possess mystical powers that could protect their owners.

Size: L31 (1¼ inches)
× φ24 (1 inch) (right)

Ghana

REPLICA AKOSO BEADS

These are beads made to imitate *Akoso* beads. In Ghana, many antique beads, including *Akoso*, have been replicated. Ghana is currently the largest bead-producing country in Africa, and many beads are crafted by Ghanaian artisans. The majority of these beads are made by the Ashanti, Krobo, and Ewe ethnic groups. African beads are continuously finding their way out into the world.

Ghana

The large central bead is a recycled glass bead. The yellow beads in the background are *Akoso* beads.

MIXED BEADS

This is a mixed bead necklace obtained in Ghana. The center features a large recycled glass bead, surrounded by various beads such as king beads, Dogon blue, *Akoso*, natural crystal, chevron, and American flag beads. Necklaces that combine beads from various ethnic groups are popular in the local antique bead markets. They provide the opportunity to enjoy a variety of beads in one beautiful piece.

Size: L40 (1⅝ inches) × φ37 (1½ inches) (black bead at center)

Ghana

249

KROBO BEADS

These are modern Krobo beads born from the thriving Ghanaian bead industry in Africa. These handmade beads are crafted from recycled glass.

Ghana

MODERN RECYCLED BEADS

These are flat and round recycled glass beads from Ghana, where beads like
Tiatiatio have been given a new life.

Ghana

DOGON BRONZE BEADS

These are bronze Dogon triangle beads. They are collectible beads that have been strung into a single strand. Typically, a few bronze beads are added to a glass bead string to make a necklace, as shown on the right page. Similar items can also be found in Cameroon and Nigeria.

Individual Dogon bronze beads

Size: L13 (½ inch) × H20 (¾ inch) (second from the right)

Dogon tribe
Mali

DOGON INDIGENOUS PEOPLE'S NECKLACE

These are the same type of bronze beads as those on the previous page. This necklace also incorporates Czech-made snake beads called *Sa-Kolo* (see p. 214).

Dogon tribe
Mali

DOGON PEOPLE'S OLD IRON & STONE BEADS

The Dogon people believe in the power of iron and often wear iron necklaces, bangles, and other items. On the left is an iron necklace with bells and *Conkada* beads. On the right is an iron necklace with bells and stone beads.

Dogon tribe
Mali

BAULE BRASS NECKLACE

This necklace combines brass plate beads from the Baule people of Côte d'Ivoire and antique glass beads. The brass plates are adorned with images of animals such as elephants, crocodiles, butterflies, and more.

Size: L88 (3½ inches) × H70 (2¾ inches) (elephant)

Baule tribe
Côte d'Ivoire

Sites of Major Ethnic Groups

Africa is said to be home to approximately 3,000 ethnic groups. Below are the main ethnic groups featured in this book, focusing on West Africa, along with their areas of residence.

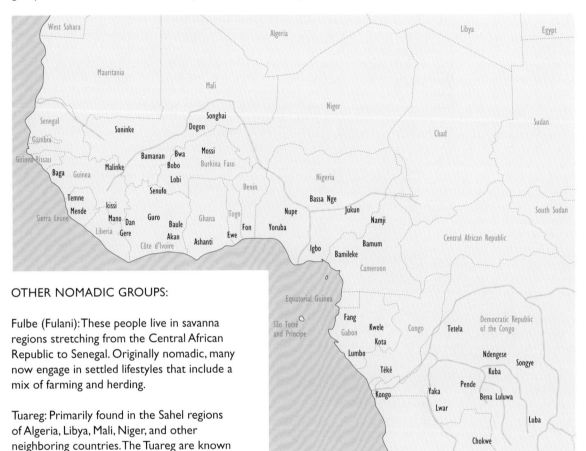

West Sahara
Algeria
Libya
Egypt
Mauritania
Mali
Niger
Senegal
Songhai
Dogon
Soninke
Sudan
Gambia
Chad
Guinea-Bissau
Baga
Guinea
Malinke
Bamanan
Bwa
Bobo
Mossi
Burkina Faso
Lobi
Benin
Nigeria
Senufo
Temne
kissi
Mende
Mano
Dan
Guro
Baule
Ghana
Togo
Fon
Yoruba
Bassa Nge
Nupe
Jukun
Namji
South Sudan
Sierra Leone
Liberia
Gere
Akan
Ashanti
Ewe
Igbo
Bamileke
Bamum
Central African Republic
Côte d'Ivoire
Cameroon
Equatorial Guinea
São Tomé and Príncipe
Fang
Gabon
Kwele
Kota
Congo
Tetela
Democratic Republic of the Congo
Lumbo
Ndengese
Kuba
Songye
Téké
Pende
Kongo
Yaka
Bena Luluwa
Luba
Lwar
Chokwe
Angola
Zambia

Only ethnic names appear.

OTHER NOMADIC GROUPS:

Fulbe (Fulani): These people live in savanna regions stretching from the Central African Republic to Senegal. Originally nomadic, many now engage in settled lifestyles that include a mix of farming and herding.

Tuareg: Primarily found in the Sahel regions of Algeria, Libya, Mali, Niger, and other neighboring countries. The Tuareg are known for their nomadic lifestyle.

Suraka: The Suraka people live in the desert regions of Mauritania and western Mali, and their livelihood centers around nomadic pastoralism, mainly with sheep.

Bwa festival

Fulani people moving cattle

Kuba funeral

Major Bead Shapes

This section introduces the basic shapes commonly used for beads.

Round
Example: *Morfia* eye beads

Oval shape
Example: Chevrons

Tube shape
Example: Mosaic beads

Double cone shape, bi-cone shape
Example: Chevrons

Abacus shape
Example: King beads

Hexagonal shape
Example: *Tiatiatio*

Dome shape
Example: Gaming beads

Cone shape
Example: Kiffa beads

Donut shape, tire shape
Example: *Dudu*, tire beads

Banana shape
Example: *Tiatiatio*

Brick shape
Example: *Tiatiatio*

Dog bone shape
Example: Dog bone

Pendant bead
Example: Mosaic beads

Flat bead
Example: Chevrons

Striped bead
Example: Watermelon beads

PRESENTED BEADS IN ACTUAL SIZE

This section introduces the actual sizes of beads presented in this book. They come in various sizes, from quite large to fairly small.

Conus shell bead
Size: L20 (¾ inch) ×
φ20 (¾ inch) ⇒ p. 28

Conus shell bead
Size: L42 (1⅝ inches) ×
φ49 (2 inches) ⇒ p. 29

Conus shell and bivalve
shell bead
Size: L25 (1 inch) × W30
(1¼ inches) ⇒ p. 30

Conus shell bead
Size: L32 (1¼ inches) ×
φ45 (1¾ inches) ⇒ p. 31

Hippo teeth bead
Size: L61.4 (2⅜ inches) ×
H43.8 (1¾ inches) ⇒ p. 37

Yoruba ivory necklace
Size: L12.4 (½ inch) ×
φ9.7 (⅜ inch) ⇒ p. 35

Cow bone bead
Size: L22.6 (⅞ inch) ×
φ45 (1¾ inches) ⇒ p. 36

Sa-Kolo
Size: L13.5 (½ inch) ×
φ20.2 (¾ inch) ⇒ pp.
38–39
Photo shows two beads.

Branch coral
Size: L23 (⅞ inch) ×
φ3 (⅛ inch) ⇒ p. 40

Mountain coral
Size: L25 (1 inch) ×
φ25 (1 inch) ⇒ p. 41

Branch coral
Size: L68 (2⅝ inches) ×
φ9 (⅜ inch) ⇒ p. 41

Djenné-Kolo
Size: L30 (1¼ inches) ×
φ30 (1¼ inches) ⇒ p. 42

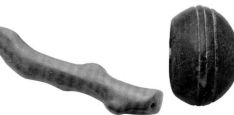

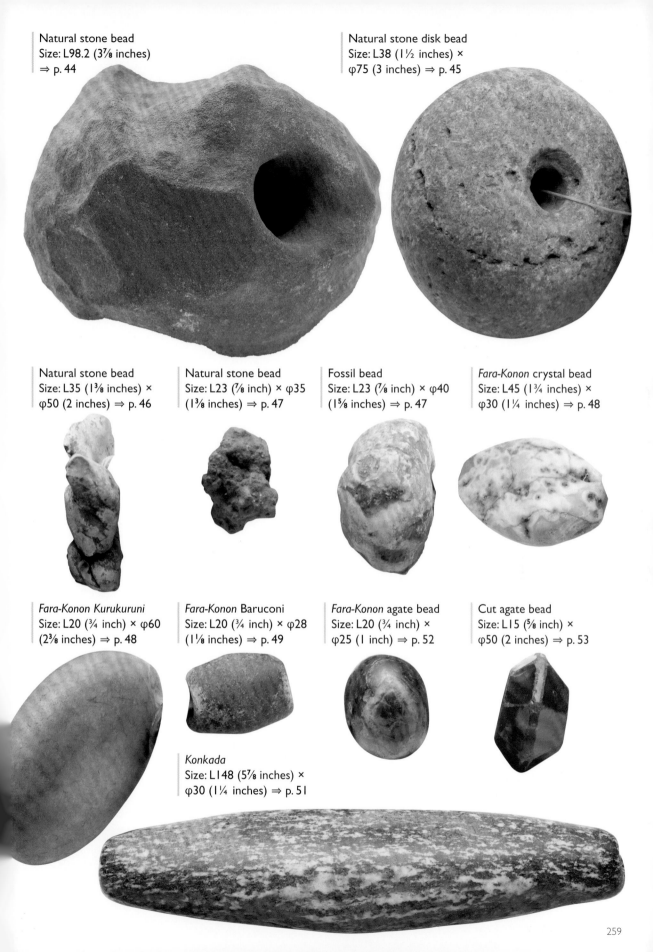

Natural stone bead
Size: L98.2 (3⅞ inches)
⇒ p. 44

Natural stone disk bead
Size: L38 (1½ inches) ×
φ75 (3 inches) ⇒ p. 45

Natural stone bead
Size: L35 (1⅜ inches) ×
φ50 (2 inches) ⇒ p. 46

Natural stone bead
Size: L23 (⅞ inch) × φ35
(1⅜ inches) ⇒ p. 47

Fossil bead
Size: L23 (⅞ inch) × φ40
(1⅝ inches) ⇒ p. 47

Fara-Konon crystal bead
Size: L45 (1¾ inches) ×
φ30 (1¼ inches) ⇒ p. 48

Fara-Konon Kurukuruni
Size: L20 (¾ inch) × φ60
(2⅜ inches) ⇒ p. 48

Fara-Konon Baruconi
Size: L20 (¾ inch) × φ28
(1⅛ inches) ⇒ p. 49

Fara-Konon agate bead
Size: L20 (¾ inch) ×
φ25 (1 inch) ⇒ p. 52

Cut agate bead
Size: L15 (⅝ inch) ×
φ50 (2 inches) ⇒ p. 53

Konkada
Size: L148 (5⅞ inches) ×
φ30 (1¼ inches) ⇒ p. 51

White striped agate
Size: L58 (2¼ inches) ×
φ23 (⅞ inch) ⇒ p. 54

Amazonite
Size: L16 (⅝ inch) × φ24
(1 inch) ⇒ p. 56

Scorzalite
Size: L28.9 (1¼ inches) ×
φ19.8 (¾ inch) ⇒ p. 59

Serpentine
Size: L55 (2⅛ inches) ×
φ28 (1⅛ inches) ⇒ p. 60

Bauxite
Size: L18 (¾ inch) ×
φ18 (¾ inch) ⇒ p. 61

Triangle bead
Size: L19.2 (¾ inch) ×
H19 (¾ inch) × D6.1
(¼ inch) ⇒ p. 63

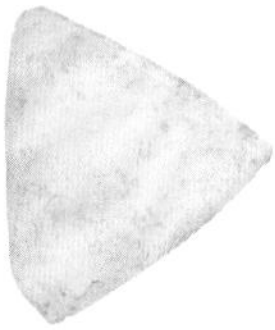

Dog bone bead
Size: L37.4 (1½ inches) ×
φ21.5 (⅞ inch) ⇒ p. 64

Amber
Size: L26.2 (1 inch) ×
φ48.7 (1⅞ inches) ⇒ p. 65

Repaired amber bead
Size: L15 (⅝ inch) × φ34
(1⅜ inches) ⇒ p. 68

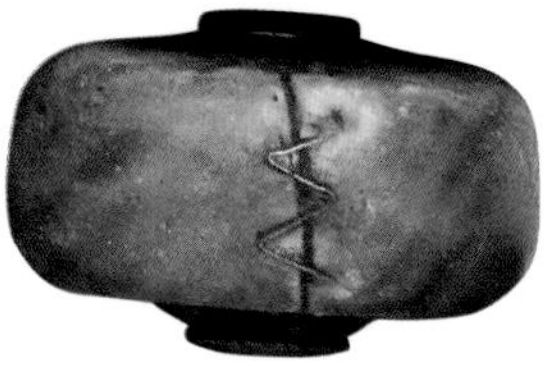

Faience bead
Size: L18 (¾ inch) ×
φ22 (⅞ inch) ⇒ p. 76

Faience bead
Size: L8 (¼ inch) ×
φ12 (½ inch) ⇒ p. 77

Nila bead
Size: L4.4 (⅛ inch)
× φ18.1 (¾ inch)
⇒ p. 79

Nila bead
Size: L4.5 (⅛ inch)
× φ9.4 (⅜ inch) ⇒
p. 80

Nila bead
Size: L4.7 (⅛ inch)
× φ10.4 (⅜ inch)
⇒ p. 81

Kamada
Size: L14.9 (⅝ inch)
× φ16.5 (⅝ inch)
⇒ p. 82

Kamada
Size: L10 (⅜ inch)
× φ13 (½ inch)
⇒ p. 84

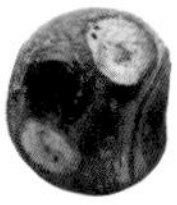

Kamada
Size: L13.9 (½ inch)
× φ16.1 (⅝ inch)
⇒ p. 84

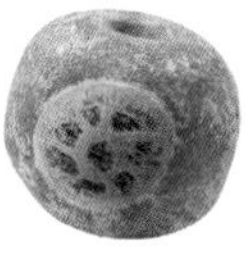

Hamada
Size: L13 (½ inch)
× φ15.3 (⅝ inch)
⇒ p. 85

Hamada
Size: L20 (¾ inch)
× φ9 (⅜ inch) ⇒
p. 85

Eye bead
Size: L25 (1 inch)
× φ13 (½ inch)
⇒ p. 86

Eyeless eye bead
Size: L12 (½ inch)
× φ12 (½ inch)
⇒ p. 86

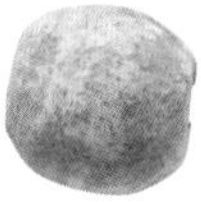

Eye bead
Size: L9.5 (⅜ inch)
× φ11.3 (½ inch)
⇒ p. 88

Eye bead
Size: L9.7 (⅜ inch)
× φ10.4 (⅜ inch)
⇒ p. 88

Eye bead
Size: L11.1 (½ inch)
× φ11.3 (½ inch) ⇒
p. 88

Mosaic eye bead
Size: L13.7
(½ inch) × φ9
(⅜ inch) ⇒ p. 88

Fakurun
Size: L17.2 (⅝ inch)
× φ12.9 (½ inch)
⇒ p. 89

Fakurun
Size: L12.3 (½
inch) × φ12.5 (½
inch) ⇒ p. 91

Fakurun
Size: L17 (⅝ inch)
× φ11 (½ inch)
⇒ p. 91

Morfia eye bead
Size: L16 (⅝ inch)
× φ16 (⅝ inch)
⇒ p. 92

Morfia
Size: L17 (⅝ inch)
× φ18 (¾ inch)
⇒ p. 93

Morfia
Size: L16 (⅝ inch)
× φ19 (¾ inch) ⇒
p. 93

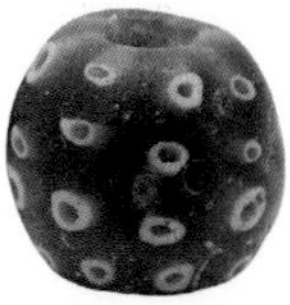

Feather bead
Size: L36.9
(1½ inches) × φ11.3
(½ inch) ⇒ p. 94

Feather bead
Size: L15 (⅝ inch)
× φ10 (⅜ inch)
⇒ p. 94

Feather bead
Size: L13 (½ inch)
× φ15 (⅝ inch)
⇒ p. 95

Feather bead
Size: L17 (⅝ inch)
× φ11 (½ inch) ⇒
p. 95

Mosaic tapestry bead
Size: L14.5 (⅝ inch)
× φ11.6 (½ inch) ⇒
p. 96

Mosaic bead
Size: L7.5 (¼
inch) × φ10.7 (⅜
inch) ⇒ p. 96

Mosaic bead
Size: L12 (½ inch)
× φ8.6 (⅜ inch) ⇒
p. 97

Mosaic bead
Size: 19.2 (¾ inch)
× φ10.5 (⅜ inch)
⇒ p. 97

Mosaic bead
Size: L16 (⅝ inch)
× φ6 (¼ inch) ⇒
p. 98

Mosaic bead
Size: L16 (⅝ inch)
× φ7 (¼ inch) ⇒
p. 98

   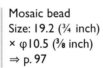

Mosaic bead
Size: L12.6 (½ inch)
× φ8.4 (⅜ inch) ⇒
p. 98

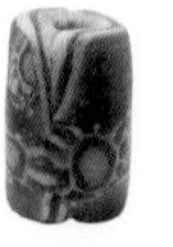

Turquoise eye bead
Size: L16.2 (⅝ inch)
× H10.8 (⅜ inch) ×
D7.2 (¼ inch)
⇒ p. 99

Mosaic wave
pattern bead
Size: L18 (¾ inch)
× φ11 (½ inch)
⇒ p. 99

Mosaic bead
Size: L19.2 (¾ inch)
× H25.2 (1 inch) ×
D4.2 (⅛ inch) ⇒
p. 100

Mosaic bead
Size: L18.5 (¾ inch) ×
H26.2 (1 inch) × D3.8
(⅛ inch) ⇒ p. 100

Twisted bead
Size: L10.5 (⅜ inch)
× H8 (¼ inch)
× D3.2 (⅛ inch)
⇒ p. 101

Dot bead
Size: L19 (¾ inch)
× H22 (⅞ inch)
⇒ p. 101

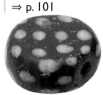

Eye bead
Size: L11 (½ inch)
× φ19 (¾ inch)
⇒ p. 101

Eye bead
Size: L11.8
(½ inch) × φ17.4
(¾ inch) ⇒ p. 102

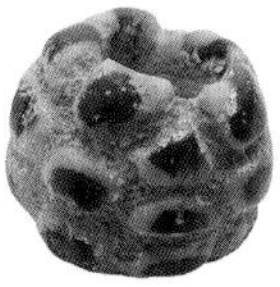

Eye bead
Size: L7 (¼ inch)
× φ9 (⅜ inch)
⇒ p. 102

Mosaic eye bead
Size: L13.3
(½ inch) × φ15.6
(⅝ inch) ⇒ p. 103

Face bead
Size: L6.5 (¼ inch)
× φ9.1 (⅜ inch)
⇒ p. 103

Eye bead
Size: L8.7 (⅜ inch)
× φ12.7 (½ inch)
⇒ p. 104

Gaming bead
Size: L12.9 (½ inch)
× φ19 (¾ inch)
⇒ p. 104

Hebron bead
Size: L17 (⅝ inch)
× φ20 (¾ inch)
⇒ p. 105

Typical chevron
Size: L30 (1¼ inches) ×
φ22 (⅞ inch) ⇒ p. 124

Typical chevron
Size: L50 (2 inch) × φ30
(1¼ inches) ⇒ p. 124

Genesis chevron
Size: L42.7 (1⅝ inches)
× φ30.6 (1¼ inches)
⇒ p. 124

Hexagonal chevron
Size: L32 (1¼ inches) ×
φ13 (½ inch) ⇒ p. 126

Typical chevron
Size: L42 (1⅝ inches) ×
φ32 (1¼ inches) ⇒ p. 127

Cut chevron
Size: L38 (1½ inches) × φ17
(⅝ inch) ⇒ p. 128

Cut chevron
Size: L27 (1⅛ inches) ×
φ24 (1 inch) ⇒ p. 128

Dog bone chevron
Size: L25 (1 inch) ×
φ26 (1 inch) ⇒ p. 129

Chevron
Size: L33 (1¼ inches) ×
φ22 (⅞ inch) ⇒ p. 129

Seven-layer standard
chevron
Size: L28 (1⅛ inches) ×
φ22 (⅞ inch) ⇒ p. 130

Chevron
Size: L26 (1 inch) ×
φ17 (⅝ inch) ⇒ p. 130

Green chevron
Size: L23 (⅞ inch) × φ17
(⅝ inch) ⇒ p. 131

Black chevron
Size: L26 (1 inch) × φ20
(¾ inch) ⇒ p. 132

Yellow chevron
Size: L26 (1 inch) ×
φ22 (⅞ inch) ⇒ p. 132

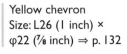

Seven-layer chevron
Size: L26 (1 inch) × φ23
(⅞ inch) ⇒ p. 133

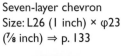

Five-layer chevron
Size: L33 (1¼ inches) ×
φ24 (1 inch) ⇒ p. 133

Collectible chevron
Size: L10.5 (⅜ inch) ×
φ8.9 (⅜ inch) ⇒ p. 134

Unique chevron
Size: L38 (1½ inches) ×
φ21 (¾ inch) ⇒ p. 134

Small chevron
Size: L10 (⅜ inch) × φ8
(¼ inch) ⇒ p. 135

Chevron flat bead
Size: L10.5 (⅜ inch) ×
φ25.3 (1 inch) ⇒ p. 135

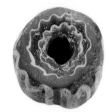

Chevron and gooseberry
necklace
Size: L28 (1⅛ inches) ×
φ23 (⅞ inch) ⇒ p. 136

Chevron wavy pattern
Size: L26 (1 inch) ×
φ21 (¾ inch) ⇒ p. 137

Chevron striped pattern
Size: L24 (1 inch) × φ20
(¾ inch) ⇒ p. 137

Chevron striped pattern
Size: L22 (⅞ inch) × φ22
(⅞ inch) ⇒ p. 138

Chevron striped pattern
Size: L21 (¾ inch) × φ20
(¾ inch) ⇒ p. 138

Chevron wavy pattern
Size: L21 (¾ inch) × φ22
(⅞ inch) ⇒ p. 139

Unique chevron
Size: L27 (1⅛ inches) ×
φ22 (⅞ inch) ⇒ p. 139

Chevron striped pattern
Size: L16 (⅝ inch) × φ18
(¾ inch) ⇒ p. 140

Chevron striped pattern
Size: L17 (⅝ inch) × φ23
(⅞ inch) ⇒ p. 140

Yellow chevron
Size: L24 (1 inch) × φ16
(⅝ inch) ⇒ p. 141

Green chevron
Size: L23 (⅞ inch) ×
φ17 (⅝ inch) ⇒ p. 141

Green chevron
Size: L25 (1 inch) × φ28
(1⅛ inches) ⇒ p. 141

Replica chevron
Size: L22 (⅞ inch)
× φ16 (⅝ inch)
⇒ p. 142

Modern chevron
Size: L38
(1½ inches) ×
φ29 (1¼ inches)
⇒ p. 143

1980s chevron
pattern flat millefiori
Size: L4 (⅛ inch) ×
φ13 (½ inch) ⇒
p. 144

Watermelon
bead
Size: L14 (½ inch)
× φ8.1 (¼ inch)
⇒ p. 146

Watermelon
bead
Size: L14.9 (⅝
inch) × φ9.2 (⅜
inch) ⇒ p. 147

Gooseberry bead
Size: L16 (⅝ inch)
× φ12 (½ inch)
⇒ p. 147

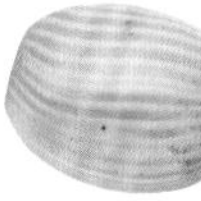

Dog bone melon
bead
Size: L13.9 (½
inch) × φ8.8 (⅜
inch) ⇒ p. 149

Brick-shaped
Tiatiatio
Size: L21.1 (⅞
inch) × φ10.2 (⅜
inch) ⇒ p. 150

Banana-shaped
Tiatiatio
Size: L33.3 (1¼
inches) × φ7.6 (¼
inch) ⇒ p. 152

Banana-shaped
Tiatiatio
Size: L47.5 (1⅞ inches) ×
φ11.8 (¾ inch) ⇒ p. 153

Tiatiatio
Size: L30
(1¼ inches) × φ12
(½ inch) ⇒ p. 154

Banana-shaped *Tiatiatio*
Size: L55 (2⅛ inches) × φ14
(½ inch) ⇒ p. 155

Banana-shaped *Tiatiatio*
Size: L59 (¾ inch) × φ13
(½ inch) ⇒ p. 155

Venetian millefiori
Size: L16.4 (⅝ inch)
× φ19.6 (¾ inch)
⇒ p. 156

Venetian millefiori
Size: L29.1
(1¼ inches) × φ19.2
(¾ inch) ⇒ p. 158

Hexagonal bead
Size: L27
(1⅛ inches) × φ9
(⅜ inch) ⇒ p. 159

Flower bead
Size: L13.4 (½ inch)
× φ16 (⅝ inch)
⇒ pp. 160–161

White hearts
flower bead
Size: L11.4 (½ inch)
× φ14.4 (½ inch)
⇒ p. 163

Venetian bead – for
European market
Size: L24.5 (1 inch) × φ16.5
(⅝ inch) ⇒ p. 164

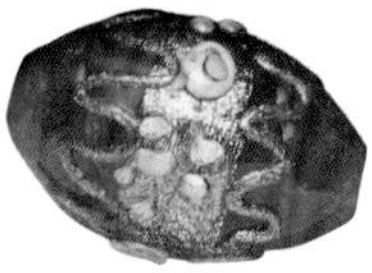

Lamp bead
Size: L28 (1⅛ inches) ×
φ19 (¾ inch) ⇒ p. 165

Venetian bead – large size
Size: L45 (1¾ inches) × φ23
(⅞ inch) ⇒ p. 165

Lace bead
Size: L99 (3⅞ inches) × φ18 (¾ inch) ⇒ p. 166

Blown glass bead
Size: L36 (1⅜ inches)
× φ20 (¾ inch)
⇒ p. 167

Wedding cake
Size: L12 (½ inch)
× φ10 (⅜ inch)
⇒ p. 168

Fancy eye bead
Size: L9 (⅜ inch)
× φ14 (½ inch)
⇒ p. 168

Tiatiatio colon
Size: L32
(1¼ inches) × φ12
(½ inch) ⇒ p. 169

Nueva Cadiz bead
Size: L36 (1⅜ inches) ×
φ15 (⅝ inch) ⇒ p. 169

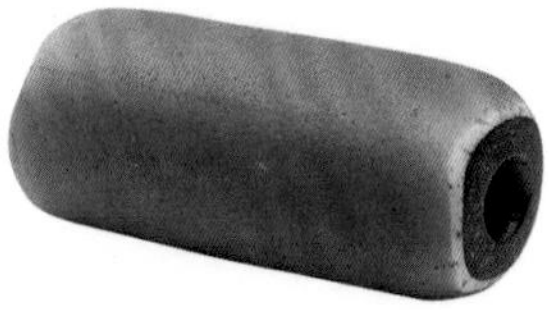

King bead – abacus
bead
Size: L18 (¾ inch)
× φ21 (¾ inch) ⇒
p. 170

King bead –
mixed
Size: L10 (⅜ inch)
× φ20 (¾ inch) ⇒
p. 171

Skunk raised dot
bead
Size: L12.7 (½
inch) × φ13.4 (½
inch) ⇒ p. 172

Yellow skunk
raised dot bead
Size: L20 (¾ inch)
× φ20 (¾ inch)
⇒ p. 173

Dot bead
Size: L6.4 (¼
inch) × φ11.2 (½
inch) ⇒ p. 174

Feather bead
Size: L14.8
(⅝ inch) × φ8.6
(⅜ inch) ⇒ p. 175

Feather bead
Size: L17 (⅝ inch)
× φ8 (¼ inch)
⇒ p. 176

New feather bead
Size: L26 (1 inch)
× φ11.7 (½ inch)
⇒ p. 177

Ghost bead
Size: L16 (⅝ inch)
× φ9 (⅜ inch)
⇒ p. 178

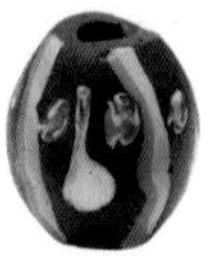

Face bead
Size: L24 (1 inch)
× φ8 (¼ inch)
⇒ p. 178

Face bead
Size: L15.1
(⅝ inch) × φ17.1
(⅝ inch) ⇒ p. 179

Dudu
Size: L39.3
(1½ inches) ×
φ22.7 (⅞ inch)
⇒ p. 181

Dudu
Size: L28
(1⅛ inches) ×
φ20.9 (¾ inch)
⇒ p. 182

Dudu
Size: L5.9 (¼ inch)
× φ11.3 (½ inch)
⇒ p. 184

Dudu
Size: L20 (¾ inch)
× φ23 (⅞ inch)
⇒ p. 185

Dudu
Size: L27
(1⅛ inches) × φ14
(½ inch) ⇒ p. 186

Dudu
Size: L7 (¼ inch)
× φ10 (⅜ inch)
⇒ p. 186

Dudu
Size: L17.8 (¾ inch)
× φ24.3 (1 inch)
⇒ p. 187

Dudu
Size: L20.7 (¾ inch)
× φ24.1 (1 inch)
⇒ p. 188

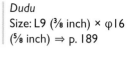

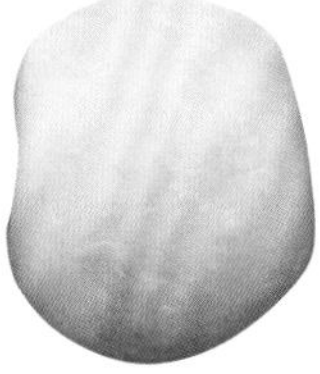

Dudu
Size: L9 (⅜ inch) × φ16
(⅝ inch) ⇒ p. 189

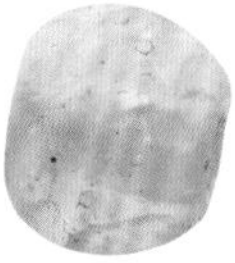

Dogon donuts
Size: L4 (⅛ inch) ×
φ13 (½ inch) ⇒
p. 190
Photo shows three
beads

Dogon donuts
Size: L4.7 (⅛ inch)
× φ12.9 (½ inch)
⇒ p. 191
Photo shows three
beads

Dogon television
Size: L20.6 (¾ inch)
× φ22.5 (⅞ inch) ⇒
p. 193

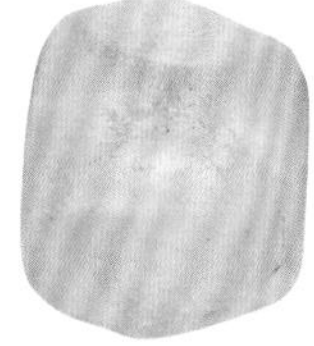

White heart
Size: L4.3 (⅛ inch)
× φ5.7 (¼ inch)
⇒ p. 194

White heart
Size: L17.4 (¾ inch)
× φ21.9 (⅞ inch)
⇒ p. 195

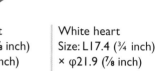

Six bead
Size: L10 (⅜ inch)
× φ11 (½ inch)
⇒ p. 196

Six bead
Size: L15.6 (⅝ inch)
× φ16.1 (⅝ inch)
⇒ p. 197

Miniyan-nuku
Size: L27
(1⅛ inches) × φ10
(⅜ inch) ⇒ p. 198

French ambassador
bead
Size: L23 (⅞ inch)
× φ18 (¾ inch)
⇒ p. 199

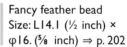

Tire bead
Size: L9.2 (⅜ inch) ×
φ24.7 (1 inch) ⇒ p. 200

Feather bead
Size: L33 (1¼ inches) ×
φ21 (¾ inch) ⇒ p. 201

Feather bead
Size: L35 (1⅜ inches) ×
φ14 (½ inch) ⇒ p. 201

Fancy feather bead
Size: L14.1 (½ inch) ×
φ16. (⅝ inch) ⇒ p. 202

Unique bead
Size: L41 (1⅝ inches) ×
φ14 (½ inch) ⇒ p. 202

Fancy bead
Size: L23 (⅞ inch)
× φ14 (½ inch)
⇒ p. 203

Fancy bead
Size: L11 (½ inch)
× φ8 (¼ inch)
⇒ p. 203

Wedding bead
Size: L23.7 (⅞ inch)
× φ13.8 (½ inch)
⇒ p. 205

Wedding bead
Size: L6 (¼ inch)
× φ12 (½ inch)
⇒ p. 206

Wedding bead
Size: L30 (1¼ inches) ×
H35 (1⅜ inches) × D3
(⅛ inch) ⇒ p. 207

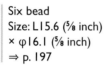
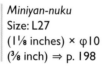
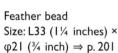
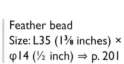

Wedding bead – Flat
Size: L12 (½ inch) × H18 (¾ inch) ⇒ p. 208

Wedding bead – Teardrop-shape
Size: L13.2 (½ inch) × φ9.2 (⅜ inch) ⇒ p. 208

Wedding bead – Standard
Size: L8.8 (⅜ inch) × φ11.9 (½ inch) ⇒ p. 209

Wedding bead – Large
Size: L28.6 (1⅛ inches) × φ17.9 (¾ inch) ⇒ p. 209

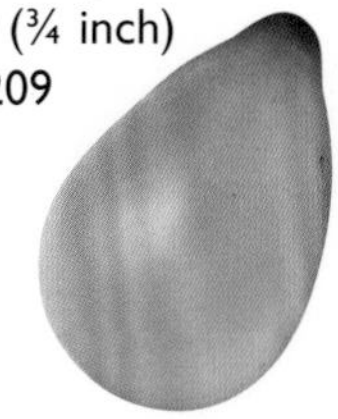

Uranium bead
Size: L5.9 (¼ inch) × φ9.6 (⅜ inch) ⇒ p. 210

Uranium bead
Size: L14.1 (½ inch) × φ15.7 (⅝ inch) ⇒ p. 211

Uranium bead
Size: L11.7 (½ inch) × φ15.5 (⅝ inch) ⇒ p. 212

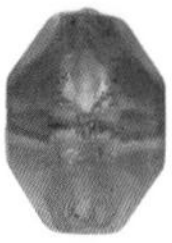

Cut bead
Size: L22 (⅞ inch) × φ14 (½ inch) ⇒ p. 213

Sa-Kolo
Size: L4.5 (⅛ inch) × φ8.9 (⅜ inch) ⇒ p. 214
Photo shows three beads

Sa-Kolo
Size: L4.9 (⅛ inch) × φ8.5 (⅜ inch) ⇒ p. 215
Photo shows three beads

Dice bead
Size: L8.2 (¼ inch) × φ7.3 (¼ inch) ⇒ p. 216

Bohemian flower beads
Size: L4.1 (⅛ inch) × φ8.1 (¼ inch) ⇒ p. 219
Photo shows three beads

Ethiopian cherry bead
Size: L22 (⅞ inch) × φ18 (¾ inch) ⇒ p. 220

Ethiopian cherry bead
Size: L27.7 (1⅛ inches) × φ23 (⅞ inch) ⇒ p. 221

Kono Fan
Size: L18 (¾ inch) × φ13 (½ inch) ⇒ p. 221

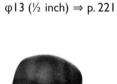

Kono Fan
Size: L9 (⅜ inch) × φ9 (⅜ inch) ⇒ p. 221

Mecca bead
Size: L33 (1¼ inches) × W25 (1 inch) ⇒ p. 222

Bohemian coral
Size: L29 (1¼ inches) × φ14 (½ inch) ⇒ p. 223

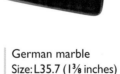

Bohemian coral
Size: L7 (¼ inch) × φ12 (½ inch) ⇒ p. 223

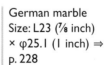

Bohemian dog bone
Size: L7.3 (¼ inch) × φ16.6 (⅝ inch) ⇒ p. 224
Photo shows three beads

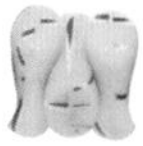

Baya beads
Size: L6 (¼ inch) × φ7 (¼ inch) ⇒ p. 225
Photo shows three beads

German marble
Size: L17 (⅝ inch) × φ18 (¾ inch) ⇒ p. 226

German marble
Size: L35.7 (1⅜ inches) × φ37.3 (1½ inches) ⇒ p. 227

German marble
Size: L23 (⅞ inch) × φ25.1 (1 inch) ⇒ p. 228

Dogon red amber
Size: L10 (⅜ inch) × φ25 (1 inch) ⇒ p. 232

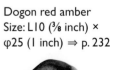

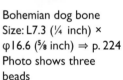

Striped copal
Size: L27.1 (1⅛ inches) ×
φ38.8 (1½ inches) ⇒ p. 230

Extra-large copal
Size: L43.6 (1¾ inches) ×
φ54.4 (2⅛ inches) ⇒ p. 231

Early vintage Kiffa
bead
Size: L14 (½ inch)
× φ14 (½ inch)
⇒ p. 242

Early vintage Kiffa bead
Size: L13.2 (½ inch) ×
H26.2 (1 inch) ⇒ p. 243

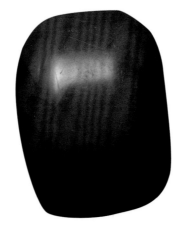

Kiffa bead: conical
shape
Size: L10.3 (⅜ inch)
× φ13.2 (½ inch)
⇒ p. 243

Kiffa bead: tubular
Size: L26.7 (1 inch)
× φ10.7 (⅜ inch)
⇒ p. 244

Drop Kiffa bead
Size: L15.9 (⅝ inch)
× W16.1 (⅝ inch)
× D9.6 (⅜ inch)
⇒ p. 244

Old Kiffa bead
Size: L7.9 (¼ inch)
× φ11.7 (½ inch)
⇒ p. 245

Kiffa bead: wave
pattern
Size: L12.3 (½ inch)
× φ15.6 (⅝ inch)
⇒ p. 245

Kiffa bead strand
Size: L13.2 (½ inch)
× φ19 (¾ inch)
⇒ p. 246

Kiffa bead
Size: L19 (¾ inch)
× H13 (½ inch)
⇒ p. 247

Bodom bead
Size: L31 (1¼ inches) ×
φ24 (1 inch) ⇒ p. 248

Recycled glass bead
Size: L40 (1⅝ inches)
× φ37 (1½ inches)
⇒ p. 249

Dogon bronze bead
Size: L13 (½ inch) ×
H20 (¾ inch) ⇒ p. 25

Baule brass necklace
Size: L88 (3½ inches)
× H70 (2¾ inches)
⇒ p. 255

Glossary

Abacus beads: The Japanese name for uranium beads.

Abacus-shaped: Beads shaped like an abacus bead.

Agate: A type of gemstone.

Akoso beads: Glass beads made in Ghana.

Amazonite: A gemstone with colors ranging from green to blue.

Amber: Fossilized tree resin, often sourced from coniferous trees like pine and spruce.

Ambroid: A type of reconstituted amber formed by heating and compressing small amber pieces.

Amulet: A talisman or charm used for protection against evil or negative forces.

Apron: Beadwork in a loincloth-like style from the Kirdi tribe.

Ashanti tribe: An ethnic group in Ghana.

Bakelite: A synthetic resin used for imitation amber.

Bamanan tribe: An ethnic group residing in western Mali.

Bambara language: The language spoken by the Bamanan people.

Bambara tribe: Refers to the Bamanan people.

Banana beads: Beads shaped like bananas, also known as elbow beads.

Banana-shaped beads: Beads shaped like bananas.

Bandiagara Escarpment: Inhabited by Mali's Dogon tribe. This area is a UNESCO World Heritage Site.

Baruconi beads: Stone beads named after *barucon*, which means barrel or cask. This is in reference to their bi-cone and tube shapes.

Baule brass: Brass jewelry preferred by the Baule tribe.

Baule face beads: Beads with a human face pattern, favored among the Baule people.

Baule tribe: An ethnic group in Cote d'Ivoire.

Bauxite: A type of natural material used for making beads.

Baya beads: Waist beads worn by women in West Africa.

Benin Kingdom: A historical kingdom that still exists within Nigeria.

Bi-cone shape: Another name for a conical shape.

Bodom beads: Glass beads made in Ghana.

Bohemian beads: Glass craftsmanship that became popular in 16th century Czechoslovakia.

Bohemian coral: Faux coral beads made in Bohemia.

Bronze beads: Beads made of bronze.

Casein: A synthetic resin made from milk.

Celluloid: A synthetic resin used in imitation amber.

Chevron: Beads characterized by their mountain-shaped cross-section patterns.

Collectible beads: Rare and valuable beads that are difficult to obtain.

Collectible necklace: A strand of beads, often of the same type, made from collectible beads.

Conical: One primary bead shape.

Conkada: Stone beads excavated in Mali.

Conus: A general term for a variety of sea snails in the family Conidae.

Copal: Semi-fossilized natural resin. Also refers to synthetic amber made from artificial resins.

Coral: A type of natural material used for beads.

Coral beads: Beads designed to resemble coral, often manufactured in the Czech Republic.

Cow bone beads: Beads made from cow bones.

Cowrie shell: One of the natural materials used in beads. Also used as currency.

Cut beads: Beads with facets or cuts.

Demba: "Mother" in the Bambara language.

Dice beads: Czech-made dot beads. Also referred to as dice beads.

Dice beads: Beads with dot patterns.

Disk beads: Disk-shaped beads.

Djenné: An ancient city in Mali's Mopti Region. Strategically important in trans-Saharan trade.

Djenné-Kolo: Beads made to resemble spindle whorls used for spinning thread.

Dog bone beads: Beads shaped like bones that dogs chew on.

Dogon television: Large, cut Dogon beads.

Dogon tribe: An ethnic group in Mali.

Dome-shaped beads: Beads with a dome shape. Common in gaming beads.

Donut-shaped beads: Beads shaped like donuts. Also known as tire-shaped beads.

Dot beads: Beads with dot patterns.

Double cone-shaped: Beads with cone-shaped ends.

Dudu: Representative dragonfly beads of the Dogon tribe.

Elbow beads: Beads with a curved shape resembling an elbow. Also known as banana beads.

Ethiopian cherry: Red beads found in Ethiopia.

Eye beads: Beads designed with an "eye" motif, often created for protective or talismanic purposes.

Face beads: Beads with faces or facial features depicted on them.

Faceted beads: Beads with multiple flat faces.

Faience: A mixture of fired quartz and calcium carbonate coated with glaze.

Fakurun: Beads with turtle shell patterns, used as trade beads during the Islamic Golden Age.

Fancy beads: Beads with elaborate patterns. Often from Venice and other places.

Fara: "Stone" in the Bambara language.

Fara-Konon: Stone beads.

Feather beads: Beads with patterns resembling bird feathers.

Feather pattern beads: Beads with patterns resembling arrow feathers.

Flat beads: One of the main bead shapes.

Flower beads: Beads with floral patterns.

French ambassador beads: Beads whose legend suggests they were favored by, and purchased by, the wives of French ambassadors.

Fulani tribe: An ethnic group residing in many West African countries.

Fustat: The first Islamic capital of Egypt during Arab rule. Currently exists only as archaeological remains.

Gaming beads: Beads that resemble game pieces or tokens.

Gao: Capital city of the Gao Region in Mali. It thrived as a trading city during the trans-Saharan trade and served as the capital of the Songhai Empire.

Genesis chevron: Antique beads with seven-layer chevron patterns.

German marble: Beads made from German-made glass marbles.

Ghost beads: Beads with patterns that resemble ghosts.

Glassblown beads: Beads created using glassblowing techniques.

Gooseberry beads: Beads shaped like the gooseberry fruit.

Hand of Fatima: A protective amulet found in the Middle East.

Hebron beads: Beads originating from the ancient city of Hebron in Palestine.

Hexagonal beads: Beads with a hexagonal shape.

Hippo teeth beads: Beads made from shells resembling hippopotamus teeth.

Hourglass beads: Beads that resemble an hourglass or sand timer.

Java beads: Beads unearthed on Java in Indonesia.

Kadjolo beads: The Dogon tribe's term for transparent *Dudu* beads.

Kamada: A type of eye bead found in Djenné.

Kiffa beads: Recycled glass beads made in Kiffa, Mauritania.

King beads: Beads preferred by high-status individuals in Ghana and Côte d'Ivoire.

Kirdi tribe: A tribe in Cameroon.

Kolon: In the Bambara language this term refers to cowrie shells.

Khomeisa: Accessories used by the Tuareg people as protective talismans.

Kono-Fan: Red beads found in West Africa. Means "pigeon's egg." Similar to Ethiopian Cherry beads.

Konon: In the Bambara language this term refers to glass beads.

Krobo tribe: An ethnic group in Ghana.

Kuba cloth: Geometric-patterned fabric made by the Kuba people using raffia palm fibers.

Kuba tribe: An ethnic group in the Democratic Republic of the Congo.

Kurkurni beads: Small stone beads with holes drilled slightly off-center.

Lace beads: Venetian beads with lace-like patterns.

Lampwork beads: Beads created one by one through lampworking techniques.

Lampworking: A type of torchworking.

Lost-wax casting: A casting technique that uses wax models to create a mold for casting metal or other materials.

Love beads: Waist beads used by African women to express feminism and other cultural meanings. These include Baya beads, among others.

Maasai people: Indigenous people living in the southern part of Kenya and the northern part of Tanzania.

Manik Pelangi: Glass beads found on the island of Java. Similar to Morfia beads.

Mecca beads: Beads worn as a symbol of having completed the pilgrimage to Mecca.

Melon beads: Antique Venetian beads known for their distinctive melon-like stripes.

Millefiori: Means "a thousand flowers." Refers to Venetian beads.

Miniyan-nuku: Means "related to snake intestines" in the Bambara language.

Mixed beads: Beads of various kinds combined in a strand.

Morfia: Trade beads from the Islamic Golden Age excavated in Mauritania and Mali.

Mosaic beads: Beads with a mosaic pattern.

Mosaic wave pattern beads: Beads with a mosaic design that resembles waves.

Murano Island: A major production center for Venetian beads.

Namji tribe: An ethnic group in Cameroon.

Nila beads: Green and blue glass beads that came from Islamic regions and were excavated in places like Djenné and Timbuktu.

Nok culture: An ancient culture that thrived in Nigeria from around the 10th century BCE to the 6th century CE.

Nueva Cadiz beads: Beads named after the excavation site of Nueva Cadiz in Venezuela.

Onion skin: Beads with patterns that resemble onion peels.

Pendant beads: Beads with a hole for stringing.

Phenolic resin: A synthetic resin used for imitation amber.

Pillow amber beads: Diamond-shaped beads of repaired amber.

Powdered glass beads: Beads produced by crushing recycled glass into a powder.

Raffia: A type of fiber obtained from the leaves of palms in the *Raffia* genus. It is used in clothing and jewelry.

Recycled beads: Beads made from powdered glass. Created as part of recycling efforts.

Red amber: Refers to imitation amber made from red-tinted synthetic resin.

Repaired amber beads: Amber beads from the Suraka tribe that have been repaired.

Rosetta: The Italian name for a chevron bead.

Round beads: One of the main bead shapes.

Sa-Kolo: The Bamanan term for snake bone beads.

Scorzalite: A variety of amazonite.

Second-generation chevron: Six-layer chevron beads made in Venice.

Serpentine: A type of stone related to amazonite.

Shell beads: Beads made from shells.

Six beads: Beads with patterns resembling the numeral 6; also known as Zen beads.

Skunk raised dot beads: Beads inspired by a skunk's patterning.

Snake bone beads: Beads made to resemble snake bones, whether made from glass, metal, or other materials.

Sokinan: Another name for wedding beads.

Songhai Empire: An Islamic empire in West Africa that emerged in the 15th century.

Soninke tribe: A people of Mali and the Republic of Senegal.

Standard chevron: Venetian-made chevron beads from the colonial era.

Stone beads: A type of bead made from natural materials.

Strand: Refers to multiple beads of the same kind strung together on a cord or thread.

Striped beads: Beads with striped patterns.

Suraka tribe: A people living in the Sahara Desert and practicing nomadic pastoralism in the western regions of Mauritania and Mali.

Synthetic amber: Imitation amber made from synthetic resins.

Tapestry beads: Beads with a pattern that resembles a tapestry.

Thousand dot beads: Beads with fine dot patterns.

Tiatiatio: Millefiori in Bambara language.

Tie-konon: Chevron beads in the Bambara language.

Timbuktu: A city in the midstream region of the Niger River in Mali. Known for its historical significance during the Mali Empire and Songhai Empire.

Tire bead family: Three types of beads preferred by the Bamanan people: tire beads, French ambassador beads, and *Miniyan-nuku*.

Tire beads: Beads shaped like a car tire.

Tire-shaped: Beads shaped like a car tire. Also known as donut-shaped beads.

Trade: Refers to "trade beads" that were used for trade between different countries and cultures. "African trade" specifically refers to beads that were traded in Africa.

Trade beads: Beads used as trade goods.

Triangle beads: Beads that are triangular in shape.

Tuareg tribe: Nomadic people in the western Sahara Desert.

Tubular: Another primary bead shape.

Twist beads: Beads with patterns created through twisting. A type of lampworking.

Uranium beads: Beads colored using uranium as a dye.

Vaseline beads: The American term for uranium beads.

Venetian beads: Glass craftsmanship that has inherited techniques from Roman times.

Watermelon beads: Beads with patterns resembling watermelons.

Wedding beads: Beads worn by Soninke women when attending weddings.

Wedding cake: Venetian beads decorated in the style of wedding cakes.

White hearts: Beads with a white center.

Yoruba tribe: An ethnic group primarily residing in southwestern Nigeria.

Zen beads: Named after the circles drawn by Zen monks. Also known as six beads.

Bibliography

Simak, Evelyn. Dreibelbis, Carl. and Dubin, Lois Sherr. *African Beads*. Africa Direct, 2010.

Picard, Ruth and Picard, John. *Chevron and Nueva Cadiz Beads*. Picard African Imports, 1993.

Liu, Robert K. *Collectible Beads*. Ornament Inc, 1995.

Tomalin, Stefany. *The Bead Jewellery Book*. David & Charles, 1997.

Dubin, Lois Sherr. *The History of Beads*. Harry N. Abrams, 1987.

Panini, Augusto and Di Salvo, Mario. *Middle Eastern and Venetian Glass Beads*. 2008.

Klenkler, C. E. *SAHARA. PRÄHISTORISCHE ARTEFAKTE 2*. Dodo Publications, 2003.

Kawada, Junzo. *Afurika no kokoro to katachi (Africa's Heart and Shape)*. Iwasaki Bijutsusha, 1995.

Kanzo Sekai no tombo dama (Glass Beads from the Museum's Collection). Tombo-dama Bijutsu Hakubutsukan, 1996.

Tani, Kazunao. and Kudo, Yoshiro. *Sekai no tombo dama (Glass Beads of the World)*. Sato Shuppan, 1999.

Ueda, Masako. and Ueda, Shinji. *Tabisuru tombo dama Traveling Glass Beads*. Seikoudoku Books, 2008.

Yuzumi, Tsuneo. *Tombo dama Glass Beads*. Heibonsha, 2003.

Bezu tunagu kazaru miseru (Beads: Connecting, Adorning, Showcasing). National Museum of Ethnology, 2017.

Ikegaya, Kazunobu. *Bezu de tadoru homo sapiens shi Tracing Human History with Beads*. Showado, 2020.

Karklins, Karlis. "Insight into the 17th-Century Bead Industry of Middelburg, the Netherlands." BEADS: Journal of the Society of Bead Researchers, Society of Bead Researchers, 2021.

Special Thanks

Masataka Kitajima
Akafa Amadou Traore
Amadou Amsala
Denou Nouh Coulibaly
Issouf Cisse
Peace corps Baba (Oumar Cisse)
Vieux Moumouni Traore

Farafina Tigne Musée de Perles

ISSA TRAORE

Issa was born in Bamako, Mali. His family has been running an antique dealership since his grandfather's time. He studied at a university in Japan and worked at a store specializing in international folk crafts called Tokyo Kankan after graduating. Subsequently, he established and manages GLOBE ART, an African art store in Aichi Prefecture, Japan.

A FIREFLY BOOK

Published by Firefly Books Ltd. 2024
Text © 2023 Issa Traore

First printing

Library of Congress Control Number: 2024935777

Library and Archives Canada Cataloguing in Publication
Title: African trade beads : their 10,000-year history / Issa Traore.
Other titles: Afurikan bizu. English
Names: Traore, Issa (Author of African trade beads)
Description: Translation of: Afurikan bizu. | Includes bibliographical references.
Identifiers: Canadiana 20240363426 | ISBN 9780228105008 (softcover)
Subjects: LCSH: Glass beads—Africa—History. | LCSH: Beads—Africa—History. | LCGFT: Illustrated works.
Classification: LCC NK5440.B34 T7313 2024 | DDC 748.8/5096—dc23

Published in Canada by
Firefly Books Ltd.
50 Staples Avenue, Unit 1
Richmond Hill, Ontario
L4B 0A7

Published in the United States by
Firefly Books (U.S.) Inc.
P.O. Box 1338, Ellicott Station
Buffalo, New York
14205

Printed in China | T

AFRICAN BEADS
© 2023 Issa Traore
© 2023 Graphic-sha Publishing Co., L

This book was first designed and published in Japan in 2023 by Graphic Publishing Co., Ltd.

This English edition was published in 2 by Firefly Books Ltd.

English language translation by Kevin Wilson

English translation rights arranged with Graphic-Sha Publishing Co., Ltd. through Japan UNI Agency, Inc. and LibriSource Inc.

Original edition creative staff

Planning & Editing, Book design: Katsuharu Takahashi (eats&crafts)

Photos: Naoto Takano

Proofreading: Zero-Mega Co., Ltd.

Editing: Naoko Yamamoto (Graphic-Publishing Co., Ltd.)

Foreign edition Production and management: Takako Motoki, Yuki Yamaguchi (Graphic-sha Publishing Co., Ltd.)